"This is a powerful book that conta[...] people and families. Kelly has captured what makes a well mapped spending plan successful. This book will help you manage your paycheck on payday. It's all about cash flow. Businesses spend millions of dollars monitoring the movement of their cash but most consumers don't understand the concept. Whether you are living paycheck to paycheck or comfortably, you will find her methods valuable. This book is a reflection of how she works with folks and her passion to help them live better lives. She has endured some of life's challenges and has lived to share them with you."
*– Chris Craighead, CFP® - President/CEO,*
*Centric Federal Credit Union, West Monroe, LA*

**Thankful**
Debt-Free including the home and building wealth!
– Paul & Kay H.

**Free of Worry & Stress**
This book is for everyone, at any age, and any income. You will experience freedom and wealth.
– Ashley Y.

"Kelly Brantley doesn't just talk about helping people get out of debt. She shows them how to do it. These pages are filled with testimonials from everyday people who were drowning in debt and now are taking vacations, building dream homes and building sizable nest eggs. Her simple-to-use plan, with proven results, is matter of fact and inspirational. Her financial wisdom and passion for people shine through in every chapter."
*– Judy Christie – Nationally-known Author & Speaker, Shreveport, LA*

**New Life – New Beginning**
For the first time, we see on paper what our financial future holds for us.
– Brad & Holly A.

"Kelly Brantley is my inspiration. Passionate, vibrant and uplifting, she brings her best game to her life's mission—to help us become debt free and wealthy. For CEO's of various industries to college students learning their crafts, and everyone in between, Kelly can develop a personal recipe for your success. Her program is easy to follow and she becomes your biggest fan! Don't miss her Flow Number concept—it removes frustration from your fiscal life and is the secret to your financial freedom. Enjoy her book, but more importantly, let her help you reach your potential."
— *Dr. Robert Delarosa – Associates in Pediatric Dentistry, Baton Rouge, LA*

### This Book – The Answer

Debt Free & Wealthy has allowed us to get this saving thing under control and experience real money success.
— Mattieu & Kristen B.

### Building Wealth

"Since our last meeting 5 months ago, my wife and I have put $8,000 into our savings account thanks to this system. It's amazing! We are just regular folks and can't wait to move on to our next financial chapter with Kelly Brantley."
— Kyle & Judith R.

# Debt-Free & Wealthy

## One Dollar at a Time

# Kelly Brantley

Published by Financial Freedom Counseling Service, P.O. Box 2295, Ruston, LA 71273-2295

Brantley, Kelly A.
    Debt-Free & Wealthy: One Day at a Time / Kelly Brantley.
    p. cm.
ISBN  978-0-692-37531-0

Publisher's Note:
This publication is designed to provide accurate and authoritative information in regards to the subject matter covered in this book. It is sold with the understanding that the publisher is not solving any financial, legal, accounting or other professional service. If the financial advice or other expert assistance is required, the service of a competent professional person should be sought out.

While the author has made every effort to provide accurate telephone numbers and Internet addresses at the time of publication, neither the publisher nor the author assumes any responsibility for errors and omissions, or for changes that occur after publication. Technology and services are constant changing and therefore might contain errors and/ or information that, while accurate when it was written, may be no longer accurate by the time you read it. Your use of or reliance on the information in this book is at your own risk and the author are not liable or responsible for any resulting damage or expense.

Versions of the Bible used are: New American Standard, New Living Translation, and the New International Version.

Printed in the United States of America

Cover designed by Ken Raney
Photography by Kevin Beasley Photography

## Dedication

I dedicate this book to my loving patient husband who inspired me to write. I love you more than words can say. Our sweet daughter who at the age of 10 told me to write a book, my parents who taught me to live a Debt-Free life, my in-laws who have loved me as a daughter and believed in me and my clients who continue to give me purpose.

# With a Thankful Heart

I am very blessed and thankful to have been encouraged by so many to write this book. First I must thank my Lord and Savior Jesus Christ for planting the seed within me then providing the water for growth. It is through Him that all things are possible.

A special thank you goes to my outstanding editor and friend Judy Christie who has walked this path by my side from the beginning and who God used to push me through this process.

Thank you to Chris Craighead, President/CEO, of Centric Federal Credit Union for your continued support as a friend and co-worker. Thank you for helping underwrite this project. Thank you for your sponsorship, believing in me and partnering with me to help Centric Federal Credit Union employees and members.

Thank you to Dave Ramsey for teaching me how to coach; to Les Nienow, a Dave Ramsey team member, who has provided me the guidance and support to become the financial counselor I am today. I would not be where I am today without your continued wisdom, love and support.

Thank you to friends and family: Lana Bullock, Becky Brantley, Colleen Durrett, Jackie Grayson, Lori McIntosh, Michelle Shively and to Dwayne & Debra Woodard for allowing me to write at "the camp" in peace.

A special thank you to those who gave me permission to use their stories and photographs: Glenn & Dianne Woodard, Tom & Burnelle Brantley, Donald R. Woodard, the late Rachel Woodard, Debra Baggett-Woodard, Robbie & Angela Jenkins, Paul & Kay Hylan, Steve & Jesse Putman, Shirley Colston, Lesley Evans, Linda Langton, Lindsay Waters, Mattieu & Kristen Bissell, Nathan & Angela Cruz Ledford, Ashley Yeldell, Dallas & Crystal Mitchell, Ashley McGee Whitehead, Richard & Salli Alexander, Ulrica Edwards, Kenya & Alex Morris, Matt & Michelle Rainwater, David Brad Moore, Brad & Holly Allen and Stan Hutchinson.

Thank you to all of my faithful clients who continue to spread the word and send me more clients. Thank you for your confidence and for your diligence in following and sticking with the program. You are the food for my passion and the reason for my success.

# Contents

# Contents

# Introduction

## Embarking on a Debt-Free Journey

A Debt-Free Tip: "Never give up, never give up, never give up."

– Winston Churchill

"And do not be conformed to this world, but be transformed by the renewing of your mind, so that you may prove what the will of God is, that which is good and acceptable and perfect."

Romans 12:2 (New American Standard Version)

I am a firm believer that everything happens for a reason and from it will come something good. It is our responsibility to make the best out of whatever challenges are thrown our way, and my family has learned that is certainly true when it comes to money.

Like so many people, for years my husband and I faced numerous financial crises, including credit card overload, medical bills and loss of jobs. But more than a decade ago, we decided we were tired of letting money control our lives, so we learned how to get out of debt. We were able to get out of debt when we thought we couldn't. Through that process, I became passionate about helping others do the same. My thoughts were, if my husband and I could do this, then anyone can.

1

That is the purpose of my "Financial Wellness" workshops, my speaking engagements, my one-on-one financial consulting work, and this book: to teach you how to pay off your bills, become wealthy, and live a Debt-Free life.

Whoever you are, these steps will work. I have worked personally with more than a thousand individual families developing financial plans that work specifically for them. I have worked with doctors, lawyers, teachers, policemen, plumbers, hair stylists, physical therapists, retirees, single moms, and more, all of different income levels from $2,000 per month to more than $40,000 per month. In the following chapters, you will find the tips that have helped clients pay off between a thousand dollars and hundreds of thousands of dollars of student loans, credit card debt, car loans, and medical bills. I have even helped a client with more than a million dollars in debt. But let's hope you're not quite in that shape yet!

My goal is to teach you step-by-step how to manage your money and how to become Debt-Free and build wealth. Regardless of your age or income, whether you have credit card debt or any other debt--or if you have no debt and want to have more money for your family--this book will give you all of the tools you need to make that happen. It can serve as a starting point to get you out of debt and build wealth for you and your family.

## *Introduction*

Many people are stuck in financial quicksand. Don't lose hope. Work through these pages to take small steps, expecting and achieving financial success.

One of my favorite scriptures is Jeremiah 29:11: "For I know the plans I have for you, declares the Lord, plans to prosper you and not to harm you, plans to give you hope and a future" (New International Version). During tough financial times, I have clung to this verse, and I pray that it will comfort you, too.

The lessons I teach have been learned through ongoing training, work with numerous clients —and dealing with personal struggles.

My life has been filled with challenges. Leaving home two weeks after turning seventeen, at the end of my junior year of high school, was only the beginning. All families have their issues, and mine is no different. But through my journey, I have learned that hard work and determination pay off, literally, at any age. The issues we face throughout life only make us stronger and provide growth.

After graduating from a South Louisiana high school and working at a Winn-Dixie grocery store for a year, I moved back home at age nineteen, just before leaving again to attend college three-hundred miles away. Twenty days before graduating from college and moving back home to New Orleans, I met the love of my life. We were married ten months later and have celebrated our twenty-first anniversary.

Our journey of dealing with financial challenges began early in our marriage. After being married for only two years, we were faced with our first financial reality check. I worked as a Human Resources Director for a manufacturing company and loved my job.

However, the hardest part of that work was when business slowed I had to lay off good hard-working people, often with families. Little did I know that after being instructed to lay off almost everyone in the company, I too would be laid off. The doors were closed, and I was left without a job.

How could this happen? Now what do I do? We had two car notes and a mortgage payment, a situation which required two incomes to cover our bills.

With no money in savings, living paycheck to paycheck, I was shocked, overwhelmed and felt like I had been punched in the stomach. I distinctly remember feeling depressed that weekend, like someone had died.

Working in Human Resources provided me an opportunity for growth in dealing with many different people in different situations. Shocked or not, I knew I had to find another job.

My new job was finding a job.

# *Introduction*

I left the house at 9 a.m. and drove from company to company filling out applications and putting in resumes until 4 p.m. every day. After six very long weeks, I went to work for a hospital in Human Resources.

Those six weeks taught us the value of having money for an emergency fund, how to cut back on spending and—unfortunately – how to charge on a credit card because we *had* no emergency fund.

Our financial rebuilding plan began with the construction of a home; five years later the birth of our daughter and four years after that, a job relocation.

A happy ending, right?

Afraid not.

Shortly after our daughter was born, she became very ill, and we were hit not only with fear but with another financial challenge.

My career was cut short and our income was cut in half.

Due to her illness, I ended up having to quit work to stay home with our precious child, cutting our income in half and reducing us to a one-income family.

We began selling our possessions like a boat, a four-wheeler and, eventually, our home.

These were growing pains for the journey. We did not know what lay ahead for our family, but we had to trust God to take care of us, while trying to figure out how better to manage our single income family.

Shortly after this we were transferred to south Louisiana for my husband's job, which turned out to be a mixed blessing. We lived in an apartment for six months, saving money, and built what would be our second home only to be transferred back to north Louisiana a year later. With a weak economy, it took six months from February until August to sell our house, which required our family to live at separate ends of the state.

Again, this challenge was financial but it was also a relational challenge. We had to learn how to live together again under the same roof when we were brought back together as a family in August. After another job-related move, back to north Louisiana and building another home, we were faced with our biggest challenge to date. This challenge overwhelmed us.

After three sinus surgeries and nearly thirty years as a welder, my husband was forced to change careers at the age of forty-five.

All we knew to do was pray. We did not know what direction to turn. The one thing we did know was we always turned to the Lord in prayer. We did not know how or when things would work out, but we had learned early on to

## *Introduction*

have faith and believe things would always work out for the best according to His plan and in His timing.

My husband is now a sheriff's deputy and loves his job, but he did take a pay cut. Time for yet another financial plan adjustment. I share our personal challenges with you because I want you to know that we too have been there. We have experienced credit card debt, medical debt, car debt and house debt along with job loss and health issues.

You are not alone, although it may feel like it. Whatever your situation, you can get out of the financial hole you are in.

Having gone through layoffs, illnesses, major credit card debts, multiple moves and job changes, my husband and I took control of our money. Frankly, we were tired of letting it control us.

We committed to spend less than we made, not to use credit cards and to learn to live Debt-Free. After facing our financial situation head on, we became Debt-Free, except for our home. Everyone's spending boils down to the choices made each and every day with each and every dollar.

This way of life relieves stress and offers opportunities we did not have when we were constantly digging ourselves out of debt: blessings such as a twenty-year wedding anniversary trip, and paying cash for a 2007 Ford Mustang to surprise our daughter on her sixteenth birthday.

Having learned how to handle our bills, I became passionate about helping others get out of debt and continue to live Debt-Free.

No one wants to live under the burden of debt.

I received a business degree from Louisiana Tech University and extensive training in financial management and opened Financial Freedom Counseling Service, which celebrated its seventh anniversary in 2015. I became a Dave Ramsey Certified Financial Counselor and started my own business to teach others how to win with money and live a Debt-Free life.

I am a cheerleader for Dave Ramsey's teachings and have continued to use what I learned from him as well as adding my own approaches. I was chosen as one of the top three (out of fifteen hundred) Dave Ramsey counselors from across the nation to speak at Dave's Enrichment training in Nashville, Tennessee, and I have been highlighted in his national marketing Master's Series campaign.

With my business, I travel throughout Louisiana, Texas, Arkansas and Mississippi doing financial wellness seminars for churches, businesses and other organizations, and I am currently offering financial advice bi-weekly on the morning news show for KNOE TV8 in Monroe, Louisiana and I am a frequent guest on KWCL 96.7 radio show in Oak Grove, Louisiana.

# *Introduction*

I write this book to show you there is hope and there is a way to live a Debt-Free life. It may not be easy, but you know what they say: "Anything worth having is not easy."

This book will:

- Provide you with the air you need to breathe in managing your finances.

- Give detailed instructions and tools on how to lay out a detailed personalized financial plan.

- Teach you how to stay Debt-Free and how to build wealth for your family.

- Remind you of God's love and guidance as you work your way through the challenges of money and life.

My mission is to provide financial counseling that will enable you to grow spiritually, relationally, and financially for every stage of your life; to encourage and teach you how to become Debt-Free; to build wealth with confidence and live each day in Financial Freedom. These are tools that can be learned, applied and passed on to the next generation: your children and grandchildren.

I am a child of God, a wife, a mother, a daughter, a sister, a daughter-in-law, a sister-in-law, an aunt, a cousin and a friend, and I consider it a blessing to be blessed with a passion for teaching others how to climb out of debt and never slip back into it. I want to inspire and motivate you to make a plan of action and move from "knowing how" to "doing now."

Make the choice to live Debt-Free. After all, it is *choice,* not chance, that determines your destiny. If you made poor money choices yesterday, you may not be where you want to be today. The choices you made yesterday, though, determine who you are today. More importantly, the choices you make today determine your success for tomorrow. People with a goal succeed because they have a plan and know where they are going.

I challenge you to ask yourself this question: "If I do nothing, where will I be a year from now?"

***We cannot go back in the past and make a new beginning, but we can start from where we are today and make a new ending.***

Take small steps and build momentum to get out of debt. It is the common things that will lead you to live a Debt-Free Life!

How do I know this?

If my husband and I can pay off ***$56,902.98*** in two years on a welder's salary, anyone can get out of debt.

Come along with me and learn to live Debt-Free & Wealthy.

# Chapter 1

## Relationships: Can't Live With Them, Can't Live Without Them

**A Debt-Free Tip: Understand *how and why* your spouse thinks differently than you do about money.**

**"He who walks with wise men shall be wise, but the companion of fools will suffer harm." Proverbs 13:20 (New American Standard Version)**

When my husband and I were more than fifty thousand dollars in debt – not including our mortgage – our family struggled with a common financial problem: too much month, too little money. This plagues most of the clients who knock on my office door and most of the people who attend my workshops. People want to get out of debt and stay out of debt. They want to live Debt-Free. So, they hold their breath and tackle a budget, but they cannot stick to it. Somehow the month gets away from them. Bills come due at odd times. A child gets sick or the dog needs a trip to the vet.

When they get paid, they jump into the stack of bills accumulating on the kitchen counter. If they have a little money left after they pay those, they feel a sense of relief and plan a reward for wiggling through another month.

But then, after their fun outing, the mail arrives with, yep, you guessed it, another bill. The car insurance. The electric bill. The orthodontist's monthly payment. With the paycheck spent, they give up and pull out the plastic, stressed out over money and feeling like they are in quicksand.

Sound familiar?

Let me help you get out of that dreaded trap with a simple program I devised to live Debt-Free, a program that uses a different type of budgeting, one that actually works for busy families stretching to make ends meet.

Instead of going with the flow when it comes to your money, I want to teach you how to use Kelly's Cash Flow System using my "flow number" plan to have enough money to cover your bills each month. The "flow number" is the key to getting out of debt and staying out of debt. It is the amount you start your budget with and it will be the amount you end with at the end of the month as we will discuss in Chapter 7.

But before we get to the numbers, let's talk about people because people should always come before money. A big factor with money challenges is relationships: The relationship we have with money and the relationship we have with each other.

**Let me give you a real-life example:**

One day an upset client came in to my office. "I just don't understand," she said. "I paid over $4,000 for Lasik eye surgery for my husband, and he still can't see things from my point of view!"

## Relationships

All too often this is how we feel in our relationships, especially when it comes to finances.

*Marriage is grand, as they say, but divorce is a hundred grand.*

So let's get this relationship thing right. We need to learn how to make our money and our relationships work together, not against each other.

About seventy-five percent of the work I do is helping couples learn how to understand each other and communicate better. Even if you're single or divorced or have lost your spouse to death, you may have found that money is the cause of stress with children, other family members, and even friends.

Why is this hard? Because we are all different and approach money differently. And as you know, opposites attract. That often causes financial conflict. Although I am not a licensed therapist, I enjoy helping clients communicate better about money.

In my work, I see two types of money managers and I like to use Dave Ramsey's titles for them: "Nerds" and "Free Spirits." I'll tell you right up front that I'm a Nerd. My husband is a Free Spirit. In most relationships, one person is a Free Spirit and one is a Nerd. Differing points of view about money are likely to arise. Even if you and your partner are both Nerds or both Free Spirits, you may find money causes stress.

I encounter three different types of relationships or marriages:

1.  A Nerd and a Free Spirit

2.  Two Nerds

3.  Two Free Spirits

When two Nerds come together, you have two people who know how to make money and can usually manage their money. However, they may find that life is boring and don't know how to let loose and have fun.

In the scenario of two Free Spirits, what happens is you often have two people who are broke and are usually bad money managers but are having all kinds of fun and deeply in debt. The fun doesn't last and transforms into financial pain.

In the scenario of a Nerd and a Free Spirit, what happens is that you have the Nerd who is often more serious about money and manages the money. The Free Spirit may have a huge heart and have lots of fun but has little-to-no interest in being the money manager.

It is important to understand the definition of the different personality types. You then can learn to work together to live Debt-Free. After years of working with clients with different personality types, I have learned that each person is different, uniquely made by God, and their characteristics can work well with others through knowledge. Take the time to learn why your spouse feels the way he or she does about money. This really helped take our marriage to a new level.

After my experience working with thousands of clients, I have learned that while no two people are exactly alike, many people share characteristics, which can help you communicate and solve money problems in your life.

Take a look at the characteristics of Nerds and Free Spirits to see if you can identify yourself. While you may not fit perfectly into one category, you will likely notice that you generally fall into one group or the other. Each has its good points and helps make the world a better place.

Nerds:

- Are list makers and planners
- Like to be early and never late
- Do not like surprises or a last-minute change of plans
- Are very businesslike
- Enjoy being the leader
- Are concerned about the details
- Worry
- Want an emergency fund so they can breathe
- Like things in order and in their assigned place
- Enjoy doing the budget and don't mind paying the bills

15

- Like to think about the long-term future

- See things as black or white

- Have a hard time accepting help from others

- Are perfectionists

Free spirits:

- Go with the flow, easy-going

- Are right on time or late

- Can be the life of the party

- Love surprises

- Are creative

- Spontaneous

- Have a sweet spirit

- Think about the present, not the future

- Have huge hearts and are very giving

- Want to help and save everyone

- Are not concerned about details

- Do not enjoy budgeting or paying the bills

- Do not like to take the lead

- Do not like confrontation

So, are you a Nerd or a Free Spirit?

## *Relationships*

If you're in a relationship, can you identify your beloved? Do any of those characteristics hit close to home?

While some people are blends, we almost all lean to one side or the other. It is funny to me when my clients come in and I talk to them about these characteristics; they look at each other, smile and ask me, "Have you been hiding in our living room?"

In working with all sorts of couples, I have found it is much easier to love someone for who he or she is when you understand why he or she is that way. As a Nerd married to a Free Spirit, I have learned to appreciate my husband and he has learned to appreciate me for our differences.

Usually, the things that attract us to one another and cause us to fall in love are the same things that tend to annoy us later in the relationship. This is clear when it comes to money.

The truth is that often opposites attract because deep down they do want to be more like the other person. Nerds wish they could be more creative and have more fun without feeling guilty. Nerds might love to worry less about the details and want to have a bigger heart. This is why Nerds fall in love with Free Spirits. They yearn to be more like the Free Spirits.

A Free Spirit often really does want to be more organized and on time. They really want to understand budgeting and how money works. They want to help us Nerds but do not know what they can do to help. They do not like confrontation, so they tend not to ask or talk about it.

Free Spirits fall in love with Nerds because they, also, yearn to be more like the Nerds. A Free Spirit loves the comfort of being taken care of by the Nerd, and the Nerd loves the feeling of taking care of the Free Spirit. This is why these relationships are the most successful.

However, differences can cause challenges, and we have to learn we will not change the other person to be exactly like ourselves. Over time a Nerd will likely learn to be more like the Free Spirit and learn how to have a little fun every now and then; over time, the Free Spirit will learn to be more like the Nerd and tighten up on some things.

It is important for a Free Spirit to realize that when he or she was young, he or she was told to eat green beans. As children we didn't particularly like green beans but we ate them because we were told to and they are good for us. This is the budget for Free Spirits; they do not want to do a budget but they must learn how because it is what is best for them. Children focus on what feels good and adults work together to have a financial plan that works.

If you do not learn to manage your money, then the lack of money will manage you and you will be forced to make decisions financially that you do not want to make, like having to sell a car or a house because you did not budget and bought something that you could not afford.

Do not fall into the trap of the "blame game." It is important for both of you to be on the same page relationally, spiritually and financially. Seek help if you are having trouble agreeing. Find a counselor or a pastor to help you walk through issues together. Consider working with a certified financial counselor or a CPA to help you get a budget that works.

## Friends and Relatives

Money is a funny thing and can change people for better or for worse.

Another important factor in money and relationships is that it is important not to let other people's thoughts or issues influence or change you or your relationships. We have been raised by different parents with different thoughts and values on how to manage money. This can make relationships and money very complex when two people from two different backgrounds come together.

We tend to do what our parents did because it is what we have seen and what we know. As adults, it is our job to realize that we are not perfect and neither were our parents. It is up to you to decipher between wrong financial decisions and right ones.

Do not try to keep up with the Joneses. Money can either help you or hurt you depending on how you choose to manage it. It must be treated with respect. Some clients have received an inheritance or a settlement of some kind, and each made different decisions regarding the money. Some chose to pay off debt, fully fund retirement for the year, build a child's college fund and add to the emergency fund. These are respectful, wise financial decisions. Unfortunately, some chose to purchase new cars, a new house and go on vacations and failed to save anything for retirement or college, and before they realized it, the money they had received was gone.

If you are disabled and cannot work, then you simply have to do the best you can with what you have. Different people are in different situations. I have seen clients who draw disability and collect food stamps each month, and the spouse who is able to work chooses to work to make a better life for the family, sometimes by working two jobs. However, I have seen clients who draw disability and collect food stamps each month and the able bodied spouse chooses not to work but complains about what they do not have and how life is not fair.

Why does work matter?

I strongly encourage clients who are able to work to do so. We all have been put on this earth with a purpose to provide service to others in some way.

## *Relationships*

Working provides the family with positive energy, a higher self-esteem and, most importantly, more income to build wealth, which in turn builds a better life for the family.

Through the years, I found that when I did not have much money, some people chose not to associate with me, but some seemed drawn to me. When we became financially successful, some people chose not to associate with me and others chose to approach me.

Money affects relationships.

Money sometimes can cause jealousy with friends and family members. If you manage your money well and get out of debt, or if people think you make a lot of money, you will find that some people are resentful and jealous. But you have to remember: this is not about you. It is about them, and they must work through their own money issues. For most people, hard work and discipline brings in more money. Those who do not work hard often fall behind financially.

You will see it, feel it and sometimes be hurt by it. It is sad that some cannot truly just be happy for you. Do not let this pull you down. Instead, focus on the positive and be a good steward of your resources. Stay focused on living Debt-Free, and do not worry about what other people say or think.

*This is your journey, not theirs.*

What is most important is how you (and your spouse if you have one) think and feel about yourself.

Part of understanding how to deal with someone else is understanding and knowing who you are. You must stand in the truth of who you are. While it is good to hear nice things from others, you do not need validation from your friends or family.

You need validation from within yourself and God. When you are doing the right thing and going in the right direction, God will validate your dreams and you will feel it from within. The pieces of the puzzle will easily come together for you. It may be in the form of money, self-esteem, gifts, growth, or wisdom. There are many different ways for your dreams to be validated.

When you do not get the encouragement you need from your parents or other important people in your life, someone else will be sent from God to fill that void. Our God is a good God and guides us every day in the way that we should go. Some days we hear Him more clearly than others, but He will continue to speak to us until we hear His words. Sometimes He has to speak several times to me--and sometimes loudly--before I hear Him but thankfully He never gives up on me and continues to speak.

Relationships can be complicated and are not always going to be easy. During these times we can mature and grow in who we are to become in our relationships. It is important to see the other person for who they really are and *choose* to love them anyway. Our relationships are about the choices _we_ make. We have all been given very special gifts, and it is our job to figure out what that gift is and give it to others. We all are one-of-a-kind and we all have different gifts to give. That is what makes this world such a diverse place.

Be patient with your spouse and see him or her for who he or she really is. They are not perfect and neither are you. You are in this relationship to help each other be better and to be all each can be. Having clarity and understanding of each other in the relationship is the key to a long, happy relationship.

While I am not a therapist, as I mentioned, clients come in to my office to talk about finances, but the meeting often turns into a relational counseling session. They blame each other, get upset, confused, ashamed, and try hard to justify why they are in the financial mess they are in. The tears start flowing from both of them because they are at their wits' end and do not know what to do and don't want to lose their marriage over financial challenges.

Once I take the time to talk to them about who is the Free Spirit and who is the Nerd and explain why they are the way they are, it brings clarity to the relationship. Once they look at it in this way, shame and blame melt away.

As I mentioned earlier, approximately seventy-five percent of what I do involves helping couples understand how the other person approaches decisions; only twenty-five percent actually involve the numbers.

When people understand the relationship part of the puzzle, the financial part tends to fall into place. It does take work, as all good things do, but it is well worth the effort. Talk to each other, listen to each other, and do not quit.

**Do Not Quit**

**When things go wrong,**

**As they sometimes will**

**When the road you're trudging**

**Seems all up hill,**

**When funds are low**

**And debts are high,**

**And you want to smile**

**But you have to sigh,**

**When care is pressing you**

**Down a bit,**

**Rest if you must**

**But don't you quit.**

**Life is strange**

## *Relationships*

With its twists and turns

As everyone of us

Sometimes learns,

And many failure turns about

When you might have won

Had you stuck it out


Don't give up, though the pace seems slow –

You might succeed with another blow.

Success is failure turned inside out,

The silver tint of clouds of doubt.


And you never can tell how close you are,

It may be near when it seems so far,

So stick to the fight

When you're hardest hit-

It's when things seem worst that

You must not quit!


--Author Unknown

# Chapter 2

## The Heaviness of Debt

**A Debt-Free Tip: Ignoring debt makes it heavy; have strength and face it head on.**

**"Owe nothing to anyone except to love one another; for he who loves his neighbor has fulfilled the law."**

**Romans 13:8 (New American Standard Version)**

Imagine being $117,000 in debt with twenty-two different creditors.

Can you feel the weight of that many bills? But what if that debt was gone in less than two years? That's the story of Robbie and Angela, an everyday couple who decided to change their spending and, thus, change their lives.

In February 2011, they had a total debt of $117,000. They had twenty-two different creditors, and they paid off eleven in the first three months totaling $38,600.

How?

First, they were committed, ready and willing to get on a plan.

Then came the hard part. Only six months before meeting with me, they had bought a fancy new pickup truck with all the bells and whistles, with a note of $655 per month. I knew this would not be an easy conversation because the truck was the husband's dream vehicle, but it had become a budget nightmare. As a financial counselor, I was compassionate, patient and understanding, during a very difficult discussion. But this was a champion couple who made up their mind and wanted out of debt.

They listed the truck for sale online on a Wednesday and sold it by Friday. The guy who bought the truck *paid cash*! What an example and testimony for this couple to witness. It showed them that big purchases can be made with cash and has encouraged them to do the same.

By January 2012, this family reported they had paid off $63,000 of debt in one year, a "life-saving" change for their family. By December 2012, they did it! They paid off twenty-two creditors, totaling $117,000 in debt and have since purchased their first home.

Robbie and Angela took the hard steps needed to get their finances in order, and it has paid off.

During the time they were paying down that $117,000, Angela drew a big circle on a poster board representing their circle of debt, then added small squares each representing $100 in debt. They hung it in their living room to keep them motivated and focused. For every $100 paid to debt each month, they would color in a puzzle piece on the circle, letting their nine-year-old son help.

What an awesome example they set for their son. At this young age he understands the importance of staying out of debt. After completing all the squares, they signed the back of it, got it laminated and presented it to me. Happy tears flowed from me and them.

This is a path you can walk, too, learning to live Debt-Free & Wealthy. This plan works no matter how messed up your finances are.

Perhaps you are like many of the people who come into my office on a regular basis, saying things like:

"I have an elephant on my chest."

"I can't breathe or take deep breaths."

"I have headaches and I can't sleep."

"I am ashamed, embarrassed, overwhelmed and scared."

## *The Heaviness of Debt*

These are statements I hear from people in debt. They also reflect feelings I personally have experienced. These are real feelings and symptoms caused by debt collectors and the heaviness of debt.

Debt collectors sometimes do not play fair. Do not let them use inappropriate practices or language. They cannot harass you the consumer, your friends, family, or employer. They cannot contact you at work if your employer disapproves. If they continue to do so, notify the creditor in writing, returned receipt requested, for them not to call you at work. When a creditor calls, he or she must identify him or herself and can only call you during the hours of 8:00 a.m. to 9:00 p.m.

A creditor cannot threaten to garnish your wages without filing suit against you. This means that you will actually be served papers in person by the sheriff's department. If you have not been served papers, you have not yet been sued. However, once you have been sued, it is in your best interest to contact them to try to work out a payment plan to get the debt paid before your wages are garnished. The maximum amount they can garnish is twenty-five percent of your wages. They cannot make contact with your employer until the suit has been filed. If any rules are broken, they can be reported to the Federal Trade Commission at (202) 326-2222 or www.ftc.gov.

Often, people throw up their hands and feel like bankruptcy is the only way out. I must say that I do not believe in bankruptcy, and out of thousands of clients, I have never recommended anyone to file bankruptcy. Bankruptcy is listed as one of the top five "life-altering" negative events that we can go through, and you need to understand exactly how it works.

**Chapter 7 Bankruptcy** is total bankruptcy and stays on your credit report for ten years. Generally, a family that files for Chapter 7 is relieved of repaying its short-term, high interest unsecured debt, along with some medical bills. After bankruptcy, however, the family must continue to make all payments on the family home, including interest, late charges and penalties, or they will lose their home. Any other debt secured by a home mortgage or home equity loan also must be repaid. Chapter 7 is NOT total debt relief. Debtors often leave bankruptcy court with heavy financial obligations.

**Chapter 13 Bankruptcy** is for those debtors who can afford to reorganize and pay money to their creditors and is the preferred choice if you have to file. It is the only way families in bankruptcy can cure defaults on home mortgages or pay defaulted car loans to avoid losing their homes and their cars. However, you must have an acceptable plan to catch up on your debt or you may not be allowed to keep property when your creditor has an unpaid mortgage or a lien on it. Debtors voluntarily agree to pay some portion of their debts over a three to five year period; however, it stays on your credit for 7 years. Despite the good faith of repaying, the reality is that two out of three do not make it through the repayment plan. This is because they fail to address the underlying problem: spending more money than they make. **Keep in mind that personal bankruptcy usually does not erase child support, alimony, fines, taxes, or student loans.**

Many have been led to believe that bankruptcy is a "quick fix" to their financial problems. This is far from the truth. Bankruptcy negatively affects your credit score for many years and can be demoralizing. It can also have a dire effect on your job, marriage and other areas of your life. In most all cases, bankruptcy can be avoided. Will it be easy? No. You know that nothing worth having comes easy but will be worth it in the end. No matter how deep the hole, there is a way out other than bankruptcy, and this can work for you.

**Will Debt Consolidation / Debt Management solve my debt problems?**

Many have fallen for the myth that debt consolidation / debt management will solve their debt problems. *Wrong.* Debt Consolidation only addresses the symptoms not the problem. Many companies promise they will lower your interest rates and payments but never let the customer know that this is done by extending your payments. Extending your debt keeps you in debt longer. When you prolong your debt payoff, you pay the lender more money, which is why they are in the business of debt consolidation.

Debt consolidation can also trash your credit. A debt repayment plan does not erase your credit history. Information about your accounts can stay on your credit report for up to 7 years. Therefore, if you apply for a mortgage, you will be treated as if you had filed Chapter 13 bankruptcy. To get your free credit report one time per year from all three bureaus (Experian (888) 397-3742, Equifax (800) 685-1111, and Transunion (877) 322-8228), you can go to www.AnnualCreditReport.com.

Most of the debt management companies act as if they are a non-profit agency, but that is not entirely true. Credit card companies often pay these agencies a five to eight percent return on the total amount of debt that you pay off.

The bottom line is many of these institutions leave clients in worse shape and with more debt than was originally placed in the program. Debt consolidation / debt management does not work because it does not address the spending and budgeting problem. Debt will reoccur. So sit back, take a deep breath, and keep reading because what I do works!

# The Heaviness of Debt

## Let's get started

Writing all your bills, due dates, and income amounts on paper is the first step to getting out of debt.

Before paying down any debt, pay for food, clothing, transportation, and utilities first. That also includes the house note or rent. By paying these things first, we can financially make it to see another day. If your bills are more than your paycheck, then you either have to bring in more income or cut out some of your expenses. Look in the mirror and see it for what it is. It is simply income versus outgo. Maybe you need to cut the cable or find a higher paying job or a second job to work on weekends. These are just a few things to help you find balance in the budget.

*Hope is being able to see that there is light despite the depth of darkness that you may feel.* Sometimes we feel like the light at the end of the tunnel is something that is going to run us over. You need to know that it is not, stay positive, and know that you can get out of debt *one dollar at a time.*

The way to start this process is to list all your debts, smallest to largest, regardless of the interest rates. Interest rates do not matter in this instance because personal finance is, as financial expert and my mentor Dave Ramsey says, eighty-percent *behavior* and twenty-percent knowledge. You will have more success at getting the debts paid off faster by paying them off this way.

33

The reason you pay the debt off faster is because the smallest debt gets paid off quickly, and you feel the reward of scratching that one off of the list and then you can focus on the next debt in line.

The following is an example of a "scratch-off debt" list:

| Company | Total Payoff | Min.Payment | Due Date |
|---|---|---|---|
| Super Care Credit | $500 | $25 | 3rd |
| Home Appliance | $8,500 | $130 | 6th |
| Major Credit Card | $12,000 | $185 | 30th |
| Student Loan | $33,000 | $100 | 8th |
| Total: | $54,000 | $440 | |

In this example you can see that Super Care Credit is the smallest debt, so you would pay minimum payments to all other debts and pay any extra income to Super Care Credit. If you have an extra $200 per month to apply to the debt, then you would pay Super Care Credit $225 instead of $25.

When Super Care Credit is paid off, you will then add that minimum payment of $25 to the extra income of $200 along with the Home Appliance Store minimum payment of $130 to pay on the next debt in line. So your payment to Home Appliance Store will be $355 per month instead of $130. You continue to apply $355 to the Home Appliance Store while paying minimum payments on all other debt until the Home Appliance Store is paid off. Once the

## The Heaviness of Debt

Home Appliance Store is paid off, you will apply $540 per month to the Major Credit Card.

Remember the only way to get out of debt is one step at a time. Eat the elephant one bite at a time. Pay off each debt one dollar at a time. You will be amazed how fast the process will go, and before you know it, you will be Debt-Free with Kelly. You will have good months and not-so-good months. That is how life works. Some months we are able to stay on track, but some months life happens. Don't beat yourself up for the things that you can't control. The children are going to get sick, the car is going to break down, and there will be times that you will not be able to apply all extra income to the debt.

As I said earlier, things do happen. Pick yourself up, stay positive and move forward. Don't wallow in negativity, or let debt cripple you. It will do nothing but bring you down. Do not let that be your story.

Work hard for a good ending. You can't go back and change the beginning, but you can start from where you are today and make a good ending.

I say it all the time: "If Will and Kelly Brantley can do this program and pay off $56,902.98 in two years on a welder's salary, then anyone can do this program."

And during that time, I was a stay-at-home mom with a sick baby.

Another story I want to share with you is about a couple who got married in 2010. Nathan and Angela had $14,000 combined debt. They met with me and implemented the financial recommendations and plan. She writes, "I am naturally a spender, so at first it was difficult for me to stick to the budget. However, after a month or so, discipline kicked in, and it started to flow. I wouldn't say we were ever perfect, but we kept chipping away at the debt mountain.

We paid off all of our debt in less than a year, and began building our savings. When we made a move to Florida, we paid cash for the entire process, which cost more than $4,000. Since becoming debt free, we've taken several Caribbean cruises, as well as other vacations, and it feels so great for the vacation to not follow us home. We recently paid cash for tickets to visit my sister in Germany, and we are living fulfilling lives.

We have built our savings up to a level that gives my husband Nathan peace of mind, especially now that he is beginning a brand new job in a new field. We are grateful for the plan, and for Kelly's advice, for helping us turn our financial situation in the path we believe God wants us to go."

## Chapter 3

## The Envelope Please: Learn How to Pay With Cash

## Debt-Free Tip: Spending with cash = Spending less and saving more

## "Good planning and hard work lead to prosperity, but hasty

## shortcuts lead to poverty." Proverbs 21:5 (New Living Translation)

My parents and grandparents, rearing families in rural Louisiana, used a simple system to manage their money; setting aside cash in envelopes to cover certain monthly expenses. Their practical tool has since become a staple for financial teachers everywhere, including Dave Ramsey, Suze Orman, and me! Little did I know that when I saw my grandmother pull out an envelope to pay cash for certain items and watch my parents pay cash for things, I was seeing the seeds for my career.

In this program, we know that planning for expenses and setting aside cash eases money worries, and you can learn to do this with The Mighty Envelopes. This is a practical, effective and inexpensive tool to use and helps you make sure you have enough money for certain monthly expenses.

How do I know this still works as it did for my parents and grandparents? Because every day my husband, daughter and I use the envelope approach. More importantly, clients tell me this simple step helps them take control, get out of debt, and stay out.

## How the Mighty Envelopes Work

This is a cash system where you fill individual envelopes each week with a certain amount of money allocated for each envelope, which we will discuss later in this chapter. When the envelope is empty, your spending is over until you are paid and can fill the envelope again. If you fill the envelope every Friday, but you run out of cash on Tuesday, you cannot go to the ATM for more money. You are out of cash, and you must wait until Friday to refill the envelope. Yes, we put actual cash in mailing envelopes.

Through this process you will learn to pay cash, not using a credit card or a debit card.

I do not want you using a credit card because you will spend more money and accrue debt, even if you try not to. You do not feel the swipe of a credit card or a debit card in the same way you feel the cash when it leaves your hand. There is something to be said about our relationship with Benjamin Franklin; we do not want to let him go. You don't have to take my word for it. Statistics show you will spend twelve to fifteen percent more when you use plastic instead of paying with cash.

Another great thing about this Simple System is that it works for both Free Spirits and Nerds. You will like the envelope system and you will see positive results from using it. The Nerds like it because they know what the limits are. Free Spirits like it because they can spend money however they choose. Typically, a Free Spirit does not like doing a budget, but this system makes it enjoyable for them.

**Name Your Envelopes**

The next step is to name your envelopes. For nearly every household, four walls are crucial to build a budget: food, clothing, transportation and utilities, which includes the house note. In our chapter on budgeting, we discuss monthly housing expenses and utilities, but food and fuel for transportation are important when setting aside cash in your envelopes because they are weekly expenses.

I recommend that you start by using the following basic envelopes:

- Grocery Envelope

- Weekend Envelope – Friday night, Saturday and Sunday

- Weekly "Me Money" Envelope – Monday through Friday

- Fuel Envelope

- Haircut Envelope

You would not use envelopes for the house note or electric bill because these are monthly expenses and not weekly expenses or a bill that you would pay in cash. Using this basic envelope system is a "keeping it simple process."

**Grocery Envelope**

While people differ on how they spend money, we all have to eat. Food is a crucial part of our budget. You must decide how much money you need each week to put in the grocery envelope for your family. Groceries are essential, and make up one of the four walls (food, clothing, transportation, and utilities) that you must take care of first, so that means that you should always buy groceries before you pay a credit card or buy something frivolous.

If you always take care of your four walls first, your house will not come tumbling down.

## *The Envelope Please*

Our family shops at a large discount store, which offers a variety of nonfood products, and I believe in keeping things simple. For me, the definition of grocery is anything except clothes, recorded music, and hunting stuff (I have to say that one for my husband).

In other words, the definition of grocery is one of the following: food, paper products, deodorant, tooth paste, hair products, dish detergent, soap, cleaning supplies, and dog or cat food. All of these items fall under the grocery section of your budget.

You now purchase these items using the cash out of your grocery envelope. This will help you not to overspend and keep you within your budget. Be realistic as you decide how much to put in the grocery envelope for your family.

For example, to say a family of four is going to spend $25 per week on groceries is not realistic. A more realistic number would more likely be $150 to $200 per week. You might try this approach in figuring grocery costs:

How many mouths are you feeding?

How many boys are you feeding? They usually have heartier appetites.

Do you have to buy diapers or formula?

Are you feeding teenagers?

You must have a plan. Make a grocery list before you go, decide what meals you plan to cook each night of the week. Stick to the list.

Trust me, if you don't have a plan, your neighborhood store does. There is a reason the bread and milk are at opposite ends of the store. The owner wants you to walk past as many items as possible, forcing you to spend more time in the store and tempting you to spend more money. I always say my grocery store puts the double-stuffed Oreo cookies on the end cap with a big sign flashing "Just for Kelly Brantley." These are not on my list, but they do make it hard for me to keep walking.

This is where discipline comes in. You must pay attention and maintain self-control when shopping. Here are a few ways to save money when grocery shopping:

--Do not go to the grocery when you are hungry. You will spend more.

--Clip coupons and shop sales.

--Consider purchasing off-brand products.

Name-brand merchants pay for better shelf position. However, the off-brand vegetables, for example, are on the bottom shelf, which means you have to bend down to get them. The good news is if you do, you will save money. Often, off-brand vegetables actually come out of the same production plant as the name brands.

42

## Weekend Envelope

The weekend envelope is a powerful envelope because it includes eating out and entertainment, and in today's society we all like to eat out and we do it often, more than we realize.

Our family is no different, and we include eating out and entertainment in the same envelope. If Kelly Brantley is eating out, that is entertainment because I do *not* like to cook. If you want to split this into two different envelopes for eating out and entertainment for your family, you can, but it makes it harder to manage, and we are all about simple, right? I like to think of the weekend envelope as the Friday night, Saturday and Sunday envelope. (We will talk about the weekly, Monday through Friday, "me money" envelope in the next section.)

## How to decide how much cash to put into your weekend envelope?

The weekend amount can be $25, $50 or $100 or any amount, but whatever the amount, it has to fit within your budget. You cannot allocate $1000 per week for a weekend of golf, concerts, eating out and such if your income does not support it. It is important, however, to be realistic about what you put in the envelope; be sure to budget enough money. A dollar per weekend will not be enough.

The power--and freedom--of this envelope comes in helping you understand the reality of your spending and keeping spending in check. Let's say you have fifty dollars; you may decide to go out to a nicer restaurant for dinner. However, if you have ten dollars left in your weekend envelope, you might choose a fast-food restaurant instead.

This keeps it real, both in deciding where to eat and what to eat. Sometimes our family chooses to eat peanut butter and jelly sandwiches at home and keep the money in the weekend envelope so that we will have more to spend the following weekend.

**Remember: You're in control of your money.**

Everyone's spending and wealth potential boils down to the choices made each and every day with each and every dollar.


**Weekly "Me Money" Envelope**

Now for the envelope that means the most to our family: The weekly "Me Money" envelope. This totally saved our marriage and it works. Since, as we discussed, one person may be a Free Spirit and one a Nerd, we have to allow leeway for differences. In our marriage, there is no doubt I am the Nerd, but my sweet, smart, loving, huggable husband is the biggest Free Spirit ever. Sometimes it is the smallest things we do that annoy our spouses.

## *The Envelope Please*

Let me share an example of a small budget issue in our family—one of those that caused a clash between Nerd – me – and my Free Spirit husband. (He encourages me tell these stories because we want to help other families.)

Each day he brought home debit-card receipts for soft drinks from his favorite convenience store. The amount was small, but this was messing up the budget.

I asked, "Why are you buying these soft drinks from the convenience store when we live less than three miles from there?"

"I like their soft drinks."

You know what I thought and voiced: *"But we have soft drinks in our refrigerator."*

His next reply: "I like their ice."

Ugh. *"We have ice."*

"But it is not convenience store ice." (Or, as my clients like, Sonic Ice.)

I know someone out there can feel my pain right now with this situation. I was working hard on our budget, and my husband's spending was adding up—plus, it was hard to keep track of the checkbook. He thought I was making too big a deal out of a daily soft drink, but truly every dollar counts. I finally was able to figure out the solution to this problem. Along came the Weekly "Me

Money" Envelope. Thank Goodness! Praise the Lord! Amen! (Can you tell how much I like this approach?)

### How the Weekly "Me Money" Envelope Works

Every Friday each spouse gets a certain amount of weekly money to put in his or her pocket for the next week. If you are single, then the weekly envelope works the same way. This is to get you from Monday through Friday. The weekly "Me Money" envelope, to get you from Monday through Friday, covers the following: your favorite coffee drink at the café you love, breakfast in the morning, lunch out, soft drinks, snacks, tobacco, and alcohol.

The weekly amount for each spouse can be $25, $50 or $100 or any amount, but whatever the amount, it has to fit your budget, and each spouse has to agree with the amount. Remember you cannot have a thousand dollars per week for your weekly envelope if your weekly income is five-hundred dollars. You also can not give your spouse five bucks each week and say, "See you next Friday." This will not work and you will not be married long. Or at least not happily married.

The amount of money you have for these "extras" has to be realistic and fit in with your efforts to stay Debt-Free. Remember: You want to budget paying your bills in full and on time, and your weekly "Me Money" envelope must be part of that plan.

If you are a Nerd married to a Free Spirit, you may want to allow him or her a little more weekly money than you give yourself. Trust me, this helps the relationship greatly and can help your spouse or partner enjoy the budgeting process more.

However, the rule is that each of you must take responsibility for not overspending. Each of you must adhere to whatever amount the two of you have agreed on.

One of the rewarding things about this system is that it helps us mature and feel good about our Debt-Free journey. While children do what feels good, adults devise a plan and follow it. As a husband or wife or as parents, it is your job to make this work and stay within budget. If a spouse spends his or her weekly money by Tuesday, can they go to the ATM and get more money? *No.* When the money is gone, it is gone.

Now, does my husband sometimes ask me for some of my weekly money and sometimes do I ask for some of his weekly money? Of course; we are married. If I don't need all of my weekly money, I am happy to share with him and he does the same for me. Sometimes I have plans for my weekly money, like when our daughter has a ballgame and I know I will need to give her some money for snacks or when I am having lunch with a girlfriend and there are times when he has plans for his money as well.

Using weekly money helps each spouse to be an adult and manage their money effectively for the family. It takes two to make a marriage work, and each being responsible for this envelope will make for a happier marriage and is a joint process to success.

I have been relieved and amazed at how much stress this one envelope removed from our relationship. The number one cause of divorce is money, and my husband and I no longer fight about money. The only thing we fight about now is driving. I think he drives too slow, and he thinks I drive too fast. So when we are together, I drive, and he sleeps, and we are both happy.

## Fuel Envelope

If you drive a car or truck, you'll need a fuel envelope. If you do not own a car, simply change this envelope to "Daily Transportation."

With the fuel envelope, you must ask yourself the following questions:

What kind of car do I drive?

Do I drive a gas saver or a gas guzzler?

Do I walk to work?

Do I ride a bike to work?

## *The Envelope Please*

Do I commute five miles to work or fifty miles to work?

How long does one tank of gas last?

How much does a tank of gas cost?

It is important to break your fuel costs down weekly for your budget. This will help you determine the monthly cost for fuel for your family.

The Fuel Envelope can be used two different ways:

- You can put cash in the envelope and pay cash when you fill up your car for the week.

- Or, use the debit card when you fill up, but you must put the debit card receipt in the fuel envelope, and keep a running total on the outside of the envelope of how much you have spent that month on fuel. This method will keep you aware of how much you are spending for fuel. This option allows you to fill up at the pump and not have to take the time to go inside and pay cash because we are usually in a hurry.

Whichever method works best for your family is the one you should use. However, if you find that you are overspending on fuel by using your debit card, you should go to the cash-only system.

If you do not own a car—either because you cannot afford one or you prefer to use public transportation – put the money for your fare in your cash envelope. I have a friend who lives in Seattle and uses public transportation to

49

avoid high parking fees. I have another friend who works in downtown Dallas and she has to pay parking fees each week; this would also need to be budgeted into the fuel envelope. Also, be sure to explore discounts for monthly parking passes.

**Haircut Envelope**

Haircut deserves its own envelope because it is usually done once a month or every six to eight weeks. It is easier to manage if you fill the envelope at the beginning of each month, then the cash is there whenever you need a haircut.

If you saw a picture of my husband, you would see that he keeps his hair cut short, as in shaved. Several years ago, I approached him and said, "You do not have to keep paying the barber $15 every month to cut your hair. I can do it."

At first he balked, afraid I might mess up.

But then we both laughed. What was there to mess up? He reluctantly agreed to let me shave his head and I have been doing it ever since. We both feel good about the money we save. Do you know what a haircut at $15 per month times forty years equals? *Money!*

I share this with you because it is important to me that you know that our family is no different than any other family.

## *The Envelope Please*

Now, for the second part of the haircut story I want to share with you. I have short hair, and, no, my husband does *not* cut my hair. A wonderful hairstylist, Jackie, has been cutting my hair for more than twenty-five years, and I am happy to pay her.

But, get ready for this: My husband does color my hair for me. We do not want to spend a large chunk of money every four to six weeks for me to have my hair colored. I pay for a box of hair color, and my husband simply puts it on for me, and we save hundreds of dollars every year.

These are some of the things we do to save and manage money in our family, and they work in our marriage. I realize not every husband will let his wife cut his hair and not every wife will let her husband color her hair.

**You have to do what works best for your marriage and your family so you can live Debt-Free.**

If you have a Haircut Envelope, figure out who in your family gets a haircut or color and how much that costs each month. Do you have long hair or short hair? How often do you get a haircut? This is an expense, and the cash should be put in the Haircut Envelope on a monthly basis.

The envelope system has been a tried-and-true tool that has been used by my clients and by me personally. I recently had a client tell me that she went shopping in a boutique downtown to purchase a pair of earrings with her weekly me money, and she found a purse for $150 that she also wanted. She told me that if she had not been on the envelope system, she said she would have bought the purse, put it on a credit card and gone further into debt.

However, because she is on the envelope system, it allowed her the opportunity to stop and think it through. The good news is that when she got home, she actually found a purse in her closet similar to the one downtown.

The envelope system helps you rethink your purchases and helps prevent spontaneous spending. Most importantly, it keeps you from going into debt by charging it on a credit card.

It's simple: If you have the cash, you can buy it. If you do not have the cash, you cannot buy it. It is not rocket science. The envelope system helps you exercise discipline and make the right choices. The envelope system works and is a great tool to living a Debt-Free life.

# Chapter 4

## Learning to Set Money Aside for Non-Monthly Expenses that Surprise Us

**A Debt-Free Tip: Don't just talk about saving for Christmas, vacations and hobbies. Do it!**

**"In all labor there is profit, but mere talk leads only to poverty."**

**Proverbs 14:23 (New American Standard Version)**

Are you sick and tired of not being financially prepared for the things you must spend money on that continues to pop up over and over?

Non-monthly expenses are things we do not pay for monthly but things we pay for throughout the year. Non-monthly items are expenses like oil changes, clothes, back to school, Christmas, gifts, vacation, pet care, home repair, and property taxes (if they are not included in our house payment).

In the budgeting process, it is critical we learn to anticipate expenses we know we eventually will need to spend money on. The danger in not planning for these categories is that it can lead to stressful credit card debt. When saving monthly for your non-monthly items, I recommend that you put the monthly total of all of your non-monthly items in a savings account and keep track of it on paper or on the computer as seen on the Savings Allocation Sheet located at the end of this chapter.

**What to tackle first?**

Examples of non-monthly expenses that can come up during a month:

- Purchasing a birthday gift for Mom

- Time to get the oil changed in the car

- Shots and flea medicine for the dog

- New school shoes for children

- Back-to-school supplies

- Christmas gifts and entertaining

- Vacations

- Home repair and property taxes (if they are not escrowed through your mortgage company)

Unless you build in money for these expenses, you are faced with hard choices when they come up. If you choose to write a check, use the debit card or pay cash. Without a plan for these things that have popped up, by the end of the month you may not have enough money to buy groceries and other necessities. You have already spent your money for these other unexpected things.

Because of this, you feel forced to put the expense on a credit card to survive. Once you choose to charge on a credit card, at that moment you become what I call "a rat in a wheel." You are digging a deeper and deeper hole for yourself and running round and round in circles because you do not have the money to pay off the credit card in full at the end of the month. The next month the hole gets deeper because you repeat the behavior, and now you are responsible for paying off the debt with interest.

Are you trying to catch your breath? Do you feel the stress? Do you feel the pressure? Do you feel like there is an elephant sitting on your chest?

This was our family's old way of living: winging it month to month and paycheck to paycheck. I believe that people are doing the best they can with what they have, but when they know better, they can do better. Planning for non-monthly expenses is a definite way to do better, and it is a rewarding new way of living.

## Oil Change/Tires

If you want to live Debt-Free, I encourage you to drive your vehicles for a minimum of ten years or 200,000 miles. That means you'll need to plan for maintenance.

Regular oil changes are necessary to keep vehicles running. Preventative maintenance is one of those things we tend to put off if money is running short for the month, but putting off oil changes will shorten the life span of the vehicle and end up costing you more in the long run. An oil change usually should be handled every three to six months, depending on manufacturers' recommendations and the number of miles you have driven. These are guidelines, so be sure to check your owner's manual or with a trusted mechanic for specifics on your car.

An oil change costs about $60 or less for most vehicles. If you put $20 per month into savings for oil changes, in three months, when it is time to get the oil changed, you will have the $60 cash to get the oil changed. This helps you better manage your money because the full cost of the oil change does not come out of the paycheck all at one time, and it doesn't mess up your regular monthly budget. This cash will come out of the savings account, out of the category named "car repair."

You may also consider saving monthly for tires and vehicle registration. It makes it easier if you have been disciplined in saving each month to pay cash when you are ready to buy new tires or pay the registration fee that is due for your car. (The Savings Allocation Sheet located at the end of this chapter can help with this.)

# *Non-Monthly Expenses*

## Clothes

Yes, at our house we budget for hunting clothes.

From work clothes to play clothes to church clothes to hunting clothes, we need to handle the recurring expense of what to wear.

Clothes can be handled with one of the monthly cash envelopes discussed in an earlier chapter or clothes money can be put in savings each month under the clothes category.

I work with families who do it both ways. For some families, buying clothes each month is a hobby, so they choose to spend a certain amount of cash each month out of their clothing envelope that they create. Some families buy clothes for a specific occasion or one time a year, so putting a little money in savings each month works for them.

As you decide how much you will need for clothing, think about the different types of clothes your family buys. Look back over the past year and figure out how much you have spent on clothes, then divide the yearly total by twelve. This is how much you need to save each month. *If your family spends $1,200 in clothes each year, then you need to save $100 per month to cover the cost of clothes for your family for the year.* This is one of those categories that we don't necessarily think about ahead of time. If planned for, it will make your shopping experience less stressful and more enjoyable.

**Back to School**

Back-to-School time is like Christmas, it comes at the same time every year. Saving just $25 per month will give you $300 in one year to spend on these annual expenses. Sending the kids back to school does not have to be a stressful time. If you have patience and do some planning, you will reduce your stress level and you will not blow your budget.

Set aside money each month so the cost of back-to-school does not hit you all at once.

Many students wear uniforms to school, whether in public or private school. Make a list of exactly what you need to buy (like how many shirts, shorts and pants you need) so you don't make unnecessary purchases.

Do not wait until the last minute. Set a specific date and time for school shopping, and give yourself a few weeks' cushion. You will have more time to look for bargains and you will not be rushed to buy everything at one time. Be sure to have your child try on clothes and shoes before making a purchase.

If your child has worn flip flops or sandals all summer, don't get caught off guard when their regular school shoes won't fit. I recommend consignment sales, especially for children, because they grow so fast, and consignment clothes are often like new and cost less. Other things you will need to include in your monthly back to school savings: school supplies and back-to-school fees.

# *Non-Monthly Expenses*

## Merry Christmas

This season does not always feel merry, does it?

*Christmas is December 25th every year and it will continue to stay the same.*

Most families I work with have the same experience each year. Dave Ramsey says that "We wait until we are eating Thanksgiving dinner and take a big deep breath, gasping for air while choking on our Thanksgiving turkey, because we *suddenly* realize there are only five weeks until Christmas. We have three kids and no money – ugh!"

Don't get caught in this trap. Christmas sneaks up on us, and sometimes that can take the merry right out of us. It is critical for you to have a plan and be prepared for Christmas. Make a list of each person you buy for and put a dollar amount by each name. You must put a dollar amount by each name because the amount you spend on your child will likely be different from the amount you spend on a co-worker or neighbor.

Add up the numbers by all the names on the list to find the total you plan to spend on Christmas. Divide this total by twelve for the amount you need to save each month. If you spend $1,200 per year on Christmas, then you need to save $100 per month so you will be able to purchase Christmas with cash and *not* put it on a credit card.

If you put Christmas on a credit card, the sad part is that the person you buy for is probably finished with the gift before the end of January and before you even get the bill for the item purchased. Also, if you put Christmas on a credit card, you will end up spending most of this year paying for last year's Christmas and with interest. Don't Do It.

Start having a Debt-Free Christmas from this day forward.

I do not have the best memory in the world, so I keep a computer list of who I buy for, how much I spend on that person and the item I purchased. This keeps me from purchasing them the same gift twice. (Let's face it; if I think it is a great gift one year, my taste won't change, and I'm likely to think it is a great gift the following year as well.)

You may be amazed to find out that most Americans buy themselves a gift while Christmas shopping each year. Do not lose focus. Do not make the mistake of buying yourself a gift unless you have saved for it. This is a time to give gifts and think of others.

Below you will find a sample of how to make a Christmas list each year and how to keep up with what you buy and for whom. This can be adapted for your gift-giving situation.

### Sample Annual Christmas List

Christmas Decorations / Food                $100

# Non-Monthly Expenses

| | | |
|---|---|---|
| Our Daughter | Shoes, Make-up, Jeans, Phone | $200 |
| Mom | Jacket & Pants | $100 |
| Dad | Saints shirt & Hedge Trimmers | $100 |
| Brother | Tool set | $50 |
| Sister-In-Law | Picture for the house | $50 |
| Grandmother | Lotion & Night Light | $50 |
| Mother-In-Law | Dress & Shoes | $100 |
| Father-In-Law | Attachment for mower | $100 |
| Aunt | Purse & Movie tickets | $50 |
| Uncle | College Shirt | $50 |
| Niece | Gift Card | $25 |
| Nephew | Toys | $25 |
| Cousin | Christmas Wreath | $25 |
| Boss | Gift Card | $25 |
| Co-worker | Necklace | $25 |
| Pastor's family | Fruit basket | $25 |
| Teacher | Candle | $25 |
| Sponsored Child | Jacket & Toy | $50 |
| Friend | PJs | $25 |
| Christmas Total: | | $1200 |

*Please remember this is only an example of who a family may buy for, what gifts they buy, and how much they may spend on Christmas. Some people spend more and some people spend less on Christmas each year.*

Just don't spend more than you can pay cash for.

Another Debt-Free tip: As your family grows, consider drawing names. This will help save money while still enjoying the spirit of Christmas. In our family, we get together for a meal and only buy gifts for the young children.

You have to develop a Christmas budget that is appropriate and affordable for your family. It is important not to get caught up in the commercial side of Christmas and remember the reason for the season. Christmas is a time to celebrate the birth of Jesus, be thankful, and simply enjoy each other's company.


**Happy Birthday**

Gifts vary in price tremendously. Often people ask me if the "Gift" savings category should be separate from the "Christmas" savings category? My answer is *"Yes."*

Birthdays and Christmas are two separate events, and we do a better job at managing our money when we save for these separately each month. Some months we may not buy any gifts or only buy one gift, but other months we may have to buy three or four gifts.

# *Non-Monthly Expenses*

May and June are tough months for everyone because we have graduations, weddings, anniversaries, Mother's Day, Father's Day, baby showers--and my birthday is May 8, by the way-☺. For our family, the month of August is a challenging month, too, not only because of back to school but because we have four birthdays that month.

Look at a calendar, and make a list of who you plan to buy a gift for each month. Go back through your list and put a dollar amount by each name, showing how much you plan to spend on that person. Add them all together for the total amount you will need for gifts for the year.

If you plan to spend $900 per year on gifts, for example, you will need to put away $75 per month in savings to have the cash to buy these gifts.

Suggestion: You may want to budget a little extra for party expenses and unexpected gifts during the year. If your child is invited to a birthday party, you will need to purchase a gift to take to the party. If your friend gets pregnant and you are invited to the baby shower, you will need to take a gift.

Below you will find an example of how to make your gift list for each year and how much you plan to spend on whom:

## Sample Annual Gift List

| | | |
|---|---|---|
| Unexpected Gifts | Throughout the Year | $50 |
| Party Expenses | Throughout the Year | $50 |

| | | |
|---|---|---|
| Dad | January | $50 |
| Nephew | February | $25 |
| Brother | March | $25 |
| Mom | April | $50 |
| Mother's Day | May | $50 |
| Graduations | May | $50 |
| Wife | May | $50 |
| Father's Day | June | $50 |
| Husband | August | $50 |
| Mother-In-Law | August | $50 |
| Father-In-Law | August | $50 |
| Daughter | September | $100 |
| Cousin | September | $25 |
| Best Friend | October | $50 |
| Co-Worker | November | $25 |
| Son | December | $100 |
| Total Gifts: | | $900 |

Please note that this is only an example of who a family may buy for or how much they may spend on gifts. Some people spend more and some people spend less on gifts each year. Develop a gift budget that is appropriate and affordable for your family. Be grateful and give yourself and your family a tremendous gift—living a Debt-Free life.

## Vacation

Would you like to take a vacation? Where do you want to go? Disney World? The beach? Grandmother's house? You may feel like you want to get away and not think about the cost. However, you need to think about where you are going and how much it will cost. If you have a plan, a vacation will serve its *real* purpose, which is for you to have a good time, relax with no worries and come home with no vacation bill because you paid for the vacation with cash.

If you go to Disney World or a similar spot, you will need more money than if you go to a relative's house. There are many advantages to a visit to Grandma's—including visiting time, a free spot to sleep and maybe some of your favorite meals and desserts.

If you will stay in a hotel or cottage, write on paper how many times you plan to eat out and how many meals you plan to cook. If you plan to cook, make a grocery list for the menu. How many nights will you stay in a hotel? You know the kids are going to want to buy a t-shirt or other souvenir of some kind. How much will you spend on souvenirs?

Don't forget to figure out how many miles it is to your destination and how many tanks of gas you will need to get there and *back*. Yes, I know we might rather not come back to reality, but at some point the vacation has to come to an end.

Another reality that should not be ignored: If you have debt, you should consider doing a stay-cation for a year or two, not going anywhere. The best vacation is the vacation that does not follow you home on a credit card. I have seen so many people refinance their houses or cars because they cannot afford the note but then turn right around and go on an expensive trip, knowing they cannot afford to take that trip. If you are behind on your house note, car note, electric bill, and your child has to have surgery at the end of the month that you do not have the money for, do ***not*** go on vacation. This totally frustrates me to watch. It is irresponsible and may even sacrifice retirement or your children's college. Priorities must be in order.

I also want to issue a warning about timeshares. Don't do it. Don't go to the meetings they offer for a free night stay or a free breakfast. It is a waste of time and they are highly trained pressure salesmen. I have many clients who have tried desperately to sell the timeshare they purchased only to find out later that it is very expensive and a nightmare to deal with. I have clients who have tried to get the companies to buy back their timeshare and clients who have even tried to give away their timeshare but to *no* avail. Don't fall into this vacation trap.

With some planning, anyone can take a little vacation. It is so important to research where you want to go, be flexible, and pay cash. You will come back home relaxed, with less stress and newfound energy.


**Pet Care**

Abby is our little Yorkie dog, and Elsie is our awesome snake-keeper-away cat. We certainly love our pets, and they have become part of our family. However, pets are not cheap, and they come with the responsibility of taking good care of them.

A few tips for budgeting for your pets: Pay for their food out of the grocery envelope. This helps keep things simple because you usually buy pet food at the same time you buy your food.

Also, if your sweet animal has to be groomed every so often, you need a cash envelope to cover this expense. Pet grooming must be budgeted for.

We must be sure they go to the vet for their shots and checkups. Other expenses include things such as heartworm pills and flea prevention medication. If your vet bill is $300 per year, you need to save $25 per month to pay that bill with cash.

The National Center for Infectious Diseases offers a variety of health benefits of owning a pet: lower blood pressure, lower cholesterol, lower triglycerides, and fewer moments of loneliness. Pets can lower stress and increase activities that ward off depression. Pets can increase opportunities for regular exercise, outdoor activities and socialization.

While there are benefits to owning a pet, be sure you can afford to take on the responsibility before bringing one home and falling in love with it. Be sure to understand the breed you are interested in and the risks that are involved. Once pets enter our home, they forever enter our hearts and are part of the family and part of the budget.

**Home Repair**

Are you Mr. Fix-It or do you call someone else to fix the problem?

If you are a home owner, you know how often things break. Trust me, if the toilet breaks, you will want to be able to have it repaired. A home repair savings category prepares you for these unexpected events. Other home expenses to think about: plants for flower beds, paint, blinds, faucets and other hardware.

A home will probably be the most expensive purchase you ever make, so you need to take care of your investment. Recently, a friend's garage door broke, her hot water heater went out, and a light fixture stopped working all in the same week. These things are going to happen, usually not all in the same week, but they are going to happen.

Fix such problems according to priority and cost. The most important and first item to get fixed in the above list is the hot water heater because no one likes a cold shower. The next item to fix would be the garage door because we do not like having to get out of the vehicle to open or close the garage physically, especially in the rain. The final item is the light fixture in the kitchen.

Of course, all of these are based on having enough cash in the home repair savings category to fix the items. However, if you do not have enough cash to fix everything at one time, only fix what you have cash for.

Sometimes people feel like renting is a bad idea and is a sign of throwing away money. If you are trying to build an emergency fund and get out of debt, then renting is the better choice because you are usually not financially responsible for things that break, such as the air conditioner.

If you own rental property, it is important to set aside a portion of the revenue you receive each month from the tenant for home repairs. As the owner, you are responsible for repairing items that may break. That means hot water heaters, heating and air, leaky pipes, and so forth.

Most people find home ownership to be wonderful, but it has its challenges, repairs being among them. Save money to handle the unexpected so that your budget won't break along with your hot water heater.

## Property Taxes

Property taxes can be a problem because they usually come due at a terrible time of the year: December 31st, right after Christmas. Ugh.

Most of the time property taxes are paid through your mortgage company, out of your escrow account. If you have a mortgage, I recommend you have the property taxes escrowed.

However, if your property taxes are not escrowed or if your home is paid for, it is your responsibility to pay property taxes on time and in full. The best way to win with property taxes is to set aside a certain amount of money in the property tax savings category each month. Then when they come due, you will have cash to pay the taxes and not get behind.

I worked with a family who got behind on their property taxes for several years. As a result, it slowed the sale of their home when they were unexpectedly required to move due to a job transfer. Failure to pay property taxes carries heavy consequences for residents, including fines, interest, property liens and, in some cases, foreclosure. To protect your family and your investment, it pays to have a plan to get your taxes paid on time.

You do not want to be behind on taxes of any kind.


## Utilities

Hot or cold, depending on the weather, the utility bill can vary greatly from month to month. One month the electric bill is up, the next month it may be down. One month the gas bill is up, then the next month it is down, and the same thing happens with the water bill. Even though these bills fluctuate from month to month, you can still do a budget. It relies on finding the balance, so simply find the average amount you spend on these utilities each month.

Let's say, for example, you choose to budget $100 per month for your electric bill. If you get your electric bill and the total amount owed for the month is $80, instead of $100, put the extra $20 in savings under the utility savings category. Then when the electric bill is $120 for the month instead of $100, withdraw the $20 from the utilities savings category. This way the $20 comes from savings and not from the paycheck you just received.

Through the years I have witnessed the financial burdens that an unexpectedly high utility bill can put on a family. What makes it more difficult is that high utilities usually come in the month of December around Christmas when winter is upon us. The secret to living Debt-Free is finding the balance, and this is what the utilities savings category can do for you.

Another option is to use the "levelized billing- level bill pay," a tool where you pay the same amount each month through a formula worked out by the utility companies. If the electric bill, gas bill, or water bill will be the same amount each month, this allows you to budget more precisely, and you will not need to use a utilities savings category as shown in the example savings allocation sheet at the end of this chapter.

**Medical Care**

No one likes to think about being sick—and health-care costs aren't fun to pay. But each individual and family needs a Medical Care saving category. Let's face it, at some point in time we all will need the assistance of a doctor and/or a hospital and we need to be prepared when that time arrives.

To know how much to save, start with the answers to these basic questions:

How much does your medical-insurance plan cost?

Is it deducted from your paycheck or do you pay it each week?

How does your medical insurance plan work?

## *Non-Monthly Expenses*

Do you pay a co-pay every time you go to the doctor?

Do you have to meet a deductible?

Do you have prescription medications to pay for each month?

Do you have dental insurance? Does it pay for preventative cleanings?

Do you have vision coverage?

Depending on your personal medical situation, you may benefit from creating a medical category for your family. I create a medical category for families I work with so they will be prepared to cover any medical issues that may come up.

Medical coverage is an especially complicated topic, and each person's financial requirements will be different, depending on your health, your plan and a host of other costs. The information I offer here, as elsewhere, is a guideline. Be sure to check with your insurance company and health-care providers for specific information.

If you have to pay a co-pay when you go to the doctor, I recommend you put back at least one copayment a month. You probably won't go to the doctor every month, but there may be some months that you end up having to go more than once. Everyone in the house may have to go if you catch something like the flu or a bad stomach virus.

I also recommend you build a medical deductible category for your family. If your medical deductible is $500 per person for up to two people in your family for example, you need to have $1000 in that category in case one or more in the family has to go into the hospital.

We do not like to think about going to the hospital, but it will happen. It helps to know you have the deductible in savings to cover those hospital bills. Be sure to match your medical bill with your explanation of benefits statements from the insurance company so you do not overpay. These statements show exactly how much is applied to the deductible, how much the insurance company paid, and how much you are responsible for. Just because you receive a bill does not necessarily mean you owe that amount on the bill. Make sure the doctor has filed with the insurance company and that the insurance company has paid its part before you write that check for the remaining balance owed by you.

## Hobbies

Our family has a hunting category and a cheerleading category. What hobbies do your family have and what activities do your children participate in?

Our daughter is a middle school cheerleader, with an estimated cost of $1,000 per year. However, we already know that when she gets to the high school level, the cost will double to about $2,000 per year. My husband and I put

## Non-Monthly Expenses

$200 into the Cheerleading Savings category from August to May to cover the cost of this extracurricular activity.

A tip: Research the cost of an activity before enrolling children. I recommend limiting each child to one activity so he or she will have time to do homework and, most importantly, time to be a kid.

Another very expensive hobby is travel sports. This can cost families a small fortune. You must think about the things that come along with traveling. Food, gas, and hotel stays. Trust me, when you are doing this every weekend, the cost really adds up. It almost counts as what I like to call "a mini weekend vacation." With this hobby you will travel almost every weekend from 100 miles to over 300 miles.

Like many Louisiana men, my husband loves to deer hunt and turkey hunt. This is his hobby and these expenses can run high. The costs involved with this hobby include the lease for land on which to hunt, hunting clothes (including camouflage gear, of course), bullets, corn and fuel. Saving cash to support his hobby helps both of us enjoy it more.

Sometimes wives resent husbands—or vice versa–because of the costs involved with a hobby. Often this resentment is not expressed until the financial burden is felt when trying to pay monthly bills.

I have heard wives through the years say, "I hate that boat," and I have heard husbands say, "I hate when she buys another antique."

Having owned a boat ourselves, we agree with the joke that the best two days are the day you buy a boat and the day you sell it. This feeling may arise whether the hobby is hunting, sewing, golf, or skiing. If you save for the hobby monthly, it helps remove resentment towards each other and the hobby.

It is also important to have a balance between hobbies and family time. If you do not find this balance, you may be left alone with only a hobby. Hobbies are to be enjoyed, but we must choose hobbies we have time for and hobbies we can afford. Do not sacrifice your family's future for your hobby.

## Plan, plan, plan

These are a few non-monthly expenses that are critical in the budgeting process. It is important that we learn to plan and budget for these expenses. You have to decide what categories fit your family.

*Planning is wisdom, and planning for non-monthly expenses is another tool that leads to less stress and allows you to live Debt-Free.*

So, let's get started coming up with your customized money plan.

## Non-Monthly Expenses

## Example Savings Category Sheet

The chart below shows the total in savings on the first of each month under the balance column. The chart shows how much money is deposited into the one savings account, on what date, then shows what every dollar is named for. On 1/1/12 $1000 was deposited and named Emergency Fund. On 2/1/12 $525 was deposited into the savings account and $30 was for Car Repair, $100 for Clothes, $25 for Back to School, $100 for Christmas, $25 for Gifts, $100 for Vacation, $25 for Pet Care, $25 for Home Repair, $25 for Property Taxes and $20 for Utilities. These add up to $525 deposited and the new total in Savings is $1525. This chart will help keep you from spending money you don't have in a certain category and will show you the name of every dollar in the savings account.

| Date | In | Out | Balance | Emergency Fund | Car Repair | Clothes | Back To School | Xmas | Gifts | Vacation | Pet Care | Home Repair | Property Taxes | Utilities |
|---|---|---|---|---|---|---|---|---|---|---|---|---|---|---|
| 1/1/2012 | $1,000.00 | | $1,000.00 | $1,000.00 | | | | | | | | | | |
| 2/1/2012 | $525.00 | | $1,525.00 | | $30.00 | $100.00 | $25.00 | $100.00 | $25.00 | $100.00 | $25.00 | $25.00 | $25.00 | $20.00 |
| 3/1/2012 | $535.00 | | $2,050.00 | | $30.00 | $100.00 | $25.00 | $100.00 | $25.00 | $100.00 | $25.00 | $25.00 | $25.00 | $30.00 |
| 3/8/2012 | | -$30.00 | $2,020.00 | | | -$30.00 | | | | | | | | |
| 4/1/2012 | $505.00 | | $2,525.00 | | $30.00 | $100.00 | $25.00 | $100.00 | $25.00 | $100.00 | $25.00 | $25.00 | $25.00 | |
| 5/1/2012 | | -$35.00 | $2,490.00 | | | | | | | | | | | -$35.00 |
| 6/1/2012 | $505.00 | | $2,995.00 | | $30.00 | $100.00 | $25.00 | $100.00 | $25.00 | $100.00 | $25.00 | $25.00 | $25.00 | |
| | | | | | | | | | | | | | | |
| Totals: | | | $2,995.00 | $1,000.00 | $120.00 | $370.00 | $100.00 | $400.00 | $100.00 | $400.00 | $100.00 | $100.00 | $100.00 | $15.00 |

## Chapter 5

## Step By Step to a Debt-Free Life

**A Debt-Free Tip:  Put all numbers on paper before the month begins to provide a visual financial plan.**

**"Wise people think before they act; fools don't and even brag about it."**

**Proverbs 13:16 (New Living Translation Version)**

## STEP 1

Write on paper the dates you will be paid during the upcoming month and the amount each pay check will be, if you get paid more than once a month. Be sure to write down the net pay, the amount deposited into the bank, not gross pay.  All budgets should be based on your take-home pay only.

If your pay varies for each paycheck, use the minimum amount you expect to receive. If you are paid a salary, your paycheck will probably be the same each time.  However, if you are paid hourly and work different hours each week, each paycheck may be different, depending on the hours worked.

The benefit of writing down your take-home pay for each paycheck is that it gives you the opportunity to see exactly how many dollars you will bring home for the month. This is the first step of putting together a budget that works.

Let's look at an example of this first step:

# *Learning*

| Who is Paid | Amount | Dates Paid | Day Paid |
|---|---|---|---|
| Husband | $750.00 | 28th | Friday-Weekly |
| Husband | $750.00 | 5th | Friday-Weekly |
| Husband | $750.00 | 12th | Friday-Weekly |
| Husband | $750.00 | 19th | Friday-Weekly |
| Wife | $900.00 | 4th | Thursday-Biweekly |
| Wife | $1100.00 | 18th | Thursday-Biweekly |

Total Monthly Income: $5,000

Now, as we all know, cash flows in and cash flows out. You must decide what you intend to spend money on, which brings us to the next step.

## STEP 2

Make a list of all monthly bills and their due dates. Examples of some bills to help you see how this works:

| Monthly Bill | Amount | Due Date |
|---|---|---|
| Donation | $300.00 | 1st |
| House Note | $800.00 | 10th |
| Car Note | $325.50 | 25th |
| Car Insurance | $110.00 | 3rd |
| Major Credit Card | $185.00 | 30th |

| | | |
|---|---|---|
| Appliance Store | $130.00 | 6th |
| Newspaper | $12.40 | 14th |
| Student Loan | $100.60 | 8th |
| Cable Bill | $75.00 | 1st |
| Water Bill | $30.70 | 22nd |
| Electric Bill | $125.00 | 23rd |
| Phone Bill | $145.00 | 18th |
| Life Insurance | $15.00 | 2nd |
| Total Monthly Bills: | $2354.20 | |

While you are at it, make a separate list of your debts, from smallest to largest--everything except the house note. This will help you as you begin to whittle away your debts, tackling the smallest first. For example:

| Bill | Balance | Minimum | Payment | Balance |
|---|---|---|---|---|
| Major Credit Card | $300.00 | $30.00 | $185.00 | $115.00 |
| Appliance Store | $1000.00 | $130.00 | $130.00 | $870.00 |
| Student Loan | $23,000.00 | $100.60 | $100.60 | $22,899.40 |
| Car Note | $30,000.00 | $321.30 | $321.30 | $29,678.70 |

When managing your money, use "the scratch-off debt list" paying off debts smallest to largest. While using this plan, all extra income is applied to the smallest debt while paying minimum payments on all others. This method allows you to get out of debt faster.

Personal finance is more about the behavior and less about the knowledge. Feeling the reward of paying off a debt keeps you motivated to get the next debt paid off as soon as possible. However, the emergency fund should always be built and kept at $1000 before applying any extra money to the scratch-off debt list.

Now that you know what you owe, let us go on. **From this point, you will begin to set aside money using the same envelope system used by my grandparents all those years ago.**

## STEP 3

Make a list of your cash envelopes and the amounts you will put in each envelope and when. Again, this will be unique to you. But to show you how it works, see the example below:

| Envelope | Amount | When to Fill the Envelope |
|---|---|---|
| Grocery | $150 | Every Friday |
| Weekend | $100 | Every Friday |
| Weekly "Me Money" (M-F) | $100 | Every Friday |
| Fuel | $100 | Every Friday |

| | | |
|---|---|---|
| Hair Cut | <u>$50</u> | Monthly |
| Total weekly envelope cash: | $450 | |
| Total monthly envelope cash: | $50 | |

Now you are ready to prepare for those expenses that do not occur each month, so follow me to the next step to living Debt-Free.

## STEP 4

Make a list of non-monthly expenses —the category and the amount. See the example below:

| <u>Non-Monthly Expense</u> | <u>Amount</u> |
|---|---|
| Emergency Fund (Build to $1000) | $150 |
| Oil change/Tires | $50 |
| Clothes | $75 |
| Back-to-School Expenses | $20 |
| Christmas | $100 |
| Miscellaneous Gifts | $25 |
| Vacation | $150 |
| Pet Care | $20 |
| Home Repair | $100 |
| Property Taxes | $20 |

| Medical | $25 |
| Hobbies-Fishing, painting etc. | <u>$65</u> |
| Total deposit into savings each month: | $800 |

## On the way to Debt-Free

Now that you have gathered all of your information, go back over your lists to make sure you have not forgotten a paycheck, a bill, an envelope, or a non-monthly expense. Be sure to include services you pay for one time a year such as a termite contract. If your termite contract is $180 per year, then you want to put $15 each month into your non-monthly savings for the termite contract to cover the once a year expense.

Your personalized, manageable money plan is coming together. You have gathered the financial information in your life—when you are paid and how you will spend your money each month.

# Chapter 6

## Building a Debt-Free Plan that Works

**A Debt-Free Tip: Learn to cash flow from week to week to stay on track financially.**

**"Prepare your work outside and make it ready for yourself in the field; Afterwards, then build your house."**

**Proverbs 24:27 (New American Standard Version)**


Now it's time to put together a simple friendly weekly distribution sheet that keeps track of spending. This friendly distribution sheet will hold your hand through this simple debt-free system and will give you the financial guidance you need to be successful. The distribution sheet is based on the days you are paid and the due dates of your bills. It will serve as the map that will lead you to a Debt-Free life and reduce financial stress more than you can imagine.

This distribution sheet, which runs from Friday-Friday, allows you to see where every dollar is spent, which will keep you on budget and living within your means. Why Friday through Friday? Because it's what we already know. Most of us have been trained using a Monday through Friday and weekend routine, from our school days to the Monday through Friday schedule, and many people work Monday through Friday as well. However, if you are paid on

Thursdays, for example, you may want to run your budget Thursday through Thursday.

When creating your friendly distribution sheet, determine if the month has four weeks or five weeks. Planning for five-week months is critical because we certainly want to eat on the fifth week of the month and must allow enough money to do so. At first glance, this may seem complicated, but you will quickly get used to planning for the extra week. As always, your money plan is customized for your paycheck amounts and your bill amounts, so do not become overwhelmed.

**How often are you paid? How do you deal with the fifth week?**

**If Paid Once a Month or only on 15th & 30th of the month**

If you are paid only once a month or on the fifteenth and thirtieth of the month, you receive the same amount of income whether it is a four-week month or a five-week month.

Uh-oh. This sounds like another case of too much month and too little money. Where will you get the money for the fifth week when your pay doesn't increase for an added week?

By planning.

If you are paid this way, you will have two money plans: a four-week plan and a five-week plan. If your monthly take-home pay does not increase with the added week (which it usually does not), you will simply make adjustments for the fifth week. It is also important for you to know that there are eight four-week months in a year and there are four five-week months in a year.

In order to have the necessary money for your envelopes during the fifth week, you will likely have to pay less on debt or put less money in savings. Note that if you are only paid once a month on the 1st, that check is to pay that month's bills. However, a lot of teachers are paid once a month at the end of the month or the last Friday of the month; therefore, then that check is used to pay the bills due for the next month. If you are paid once per month on the 15th, then your budget would run from the 15th of one month to the 15th of the following month.

## If you are paid weekly

If you are paid weekly, your monthly take-home pay for five weeks will be more than the monthly take-home pay for four weeks because you are being paid for each week that you work. You, too, will need a four-week money plan and a five-week money plan.

## Building A Debt-Free Plan

**If you are paid bi-weekly**

If you are paid bi-weekly, ten months out of the year you will use a four-week plan. Two months out of the year you will use a six-week plan, which includes your two extra checks per year. This usually happens in June or July and November or December.

Even though you are getting the extra check, you have to remember to plan for cash envelopes for those other two weeks. Therefore, your whole "extra" check cannot go to pay off debt or to savings because you still have to eat and put gas in the car during those two weeks.

Creating your friendly distribution sheet will guide you, showing your income and outgo balance. As you reflect on this process, remember you always want to spend cash and not charge on credit cards.

*If you charge on credit cards and don't pay them off in full every month, you are not living within your means.*

Remember the rat in the wheel that I mentioned earlier? Avoid this credit card trap.

**The Relief of the Friendly Distribution Sheet**

The good news is when you create your friendly distribution sheet and consistently use the envelope system and non-monthly expense category system, you will feel like you received a raise. You will learn to spend with cash, which will relieve your financial stress. This is refreshing and gives you the air you need to breathe.

Let's look at a sample friendly distribution sheet based on the paycheck and bill due dates gathered in steps one through four. While this may look complicated, it really is quite simple. Take a deep breath and read each line, considering how this might relate to your personal Debt-Free plans.

# *Building A Debt-Free Plan*

## *Four-Week Friendly Distribution Sheet*

### WEEK 1

Week 1 Income – Friday, June 28th through Friday, July 5th

**Checking Balance/Flow Number: $250.00 (explained in next chapter)**

| | | |
|---|---|---|
| Husband's Check – 28th | | $750.00 |
| Total in Checking: | | $1000.00 |

Week 1 Bills – Friday, June 28th through Friday, July 5th

| | | |
|---|---|---|
| 28th | Grocery | $150 |
| 28th | Weekend | $100 |
| 28th | Weekly "Me Money" (M-F) | $100 |
| 28th | Fuel | $100 |
| 28th | Haircut | $50 |
| 1st | Donation | $300 |
| 1st | Cable Bill | $75 |
| 2nd | Life Insurance | $15 |
| 3rd | Car Insurance | $110 |
| Total Bills Week 1: | | $1000.00 |

| | |
|---|---|
| Total in Checking: | $1000.00 |
| Week 1 Bills: | -$1000.00 |
| New Checking Balance: | $0 |

89

## WEEK 2

Week 2 Income – Friday, July 5th through Friday, July 12th

| | |
|---|---|
| New Checking Balance: | $ 0 |
| Wife's Check – 4th | $900.00 |
| Husband's Check – 5th | $750.00 |
| Total in Checking: | $1650.00 |

Week 2 Bills – Friday, July 5th through Friday, July 12th

| | | |
|---|---|---|
| 5th | Grocery | $150 |
| 5th | Weekend | $100 |
| 5th | Weekly "Me Money" (M-F) | $100 |
| 5th | Fuel | $100 |
| 6th | Appliance Store bill | $130 |
| 8th | Student Loan | $100.60 |
| 10th | House Note | $800 |
| Total Bills Week 2: | | $1480.60 |

| | |
|---|---|
| Total in Checking: | $1650.00 |
| Week 2 Bills: | -$1480.60 |
| New Checking Balance: | $169.40 |

# *Building A Debt-Free Plan*

## WEEK 3

Week 3 Income – Friday, July 12th through Friday, July 19th

| | |
|---|---|
| New Checking Balance: | $169.40 |
| Husband's Check – 12th | $750.00 |
| Total in Checking: | $919.40 |

Week 3 Bills – Friday, July 12th through Friday, July 19th

| 12th | Grocery | $150 |
|---|---|---|
| 12th | Weekend | $100 |
| 12th | Weekly "Me Money" (M-F) | $100 |
| 12th | Fuel | $100 |
| 14th | Newspaper | $12.40 |
| 18th | Phone Bill | $145 |
| | Total Bills Week 3: | $607.40 |

| | |
|---|---|
| Total in Checking: | $919.40 |
| Week 3 Bills: | -$ 607.40 |
| New Checking Balance: | $312.00 |

## WEEK 4

Week 4 Income – Friday, July 19th through Friday, July 26th

| | |
|---|---|
| New Checking Balance: | $312.00 |
| Wife's Check – 18th | $1100.00 |
| Husband's Check – 19th | $750.00 |
| Total in Checking: | $2162.00 |

Week 4 Bills – Friday, July 19th through Friday, July 26th

| 19th | Grocery | $150 |
|---|---|---|
| 19th | Weekend | $100 |
| 19th | Weekly "Me Money" (M-F) | $100 |
| 19th | Fuel | $100 |
| **19th** | **Savings Category Deposit** | **$800** |
| 22nd | Water | $30.64 |
| 23rd | Electricity | $125 |
| 25th | Car Note | $325.50 |
| 30th | Major Credit Card | $185 |
| Total Bills Week 4: | | $1912.00 |

| | |
|---|---|
| Total in Checking: | $2162.00 |
| Week 4 Bills: | -$1912.00 |
| **New Checking Balance/Flow #:** | **$250.00** |

# *Building A Debt-Free Plan*

This completes the example for a four-week month. There are always more four week months in a year than five-week months. As we discussed, the plan for a four-week month will be different than the plan you do for a five-week month because of the income and spending difference for each month. Also notice that the budget started with **$250** and ended with **$250**, which in essence gave every take-home dollar a name.

As you continue on through the next few pages you will see that we will now take a look at the lay-out of the five-week distribution sheet.

# DEBT-FREE & WEALTHY

## *Five-Week Friendly Distribution Sheet*

### WEEK 1

Week 1 Income – Friday, July 26th through Friday, August 2nd

| | |
|---|---|
| **Checking Balance/Flow #:** | **$250.00** |
| Husband's Check – 26th | $750.00 |
| Total in Checking: | $1000.00 |

Week 1 Bills – Friday, July 26th through Friday, August 2nd

| | | |
|---|---|---|
| 26th | Grocery | $150 |
| 26th | Weekend | $100 |
| 26th | Weekly "Me Money" (M-F) | $100 |
| 26th | Fuel | $100 |
| 26th | Haircut | $50 |
| 1st | Donation | $300 |
| 1st | Cable Bill | $75 |
| 2nd | Life Insurance | $15 |
| 3rd | Car Insurance | $110 |
| Total Bills Week 1: | | $1000.00 |

| | |
|---|---|
| Total in Checking: | $1000.00 |
| Week 1 Bills: | -$1000.00 |
| New Checking Balance: | $0 |

94

# *Building A Debt-Free Plan*

## <u>WEEK 2</u>

Week 2 Income – Friday, August 2nd through Friday, August 9th

| | |
|---|---|
| New Checking Balance: | $0 |
| Wife's Check – 1st | $900.00 |
| Husband's Check – 2nd | $750.00 |
| Total in Checking: | $1650.00 |

Week 2 Bills – Friday, August 2nd through Friday, August 9th

| | | |
|---|---|---|
| 2nd | Grocery | $150 |
| 2nd | Weekend | $100 |
| 2nd | Weekly "Me Money" (M-F) | $100 |
| 2nd | Fuel | $100 |
| 6th | Appliance Store | $130 |
| 8th | Student Loan | $100 |
| 10th | House Note | $800 |
| Total Bills Week 2: | | $1480.60 |

| | |
|---|---|
| Total in Checking: | $1650.00 |
| Week 2 Bills: | -$1480.60 |
| New Checking Balance: | $169.40 |

## WEEK 3

Week 3 Income – Friday, August 9th through Friday, August 16th

| | |
|---|---|
| New Checking Balance: | $169.40 |
| Husband's Check – 9th | $750.00 |
| Total in Checking: | $919.40 |

Week 3 Bills – Friday, August 9th through Friday, August 16th

| | | |
|---|---|---|
| 9th | Grocery | $150 |
| 9th | Weekend | $100 |
| 9th | Weekly "Me Money" (M-F) | $100 |
| 9th | Fuel | $100 |
| 14th | Newspaper | $12.40 |
| 18th | Phone Bill | $145 |
| Total Bills Week 3: | | $607.40 |

| | |
|---|---|
| Total in Checking: | $ 919.40 |
| Week 3 Bills: | -$ 607.40 |
| New Checking Balance: | $312.00 |

96

# *Building A Debt-Free Plan*

## <u>WEEK 4</u>

Week 4 Income – Friday, August 16th through Friday, August 23rd

| | |
|---|---|
| New Checking Balance: | $312.00 |
| Wife's Check – 15th | $1100.00 |
| Husband's Check – 16th | $750.00 |
| Total in Checking: | $2162.00 |

Week 4 Bills – Friday, August 16th through Friday, August 23rd

| 16th | Grocery | $150 |
|---|---|---|
| 16th | Weekend | $100 |
| 16th | Weekly "Me Money" (M-F) | $100 |
| 16th | Fuel | $100 |
| 22nd | Water | $30.70 |
| 23rd | Electricity | $125 |
| Total Bills Week 4: | | $605.70 |

| | |
|---|---|
| Total in Checking: | $2162.00 |
| Week 4 Bills: | -$605.70 |
| New Checking Balance: | $1556.30 |

## WEEK 5

Week 5 Income – Friday, August 23rd through Friday, August 30th

| | |
|---|---|
| New Checking Balance: | $1556.30 |
| Husband's Check – 23rd | $750.00 |
| Total in Checking: | $2306.30 |

Week 5 Bills – Friday, August 23rd through Friday, August 30th

| | | |
|---|---|---|
| 23rd | Grocery | $150 |
| 23rd | Weekend | $100 |
| 23rd | Weekly "Me Money" (M-F) | $100 |
| 23rd | Fuel | $100 |
| **23rd** | **Extra for savings or debt** | **$300** |
| **23rd** | **Savings Category Deposit** | **$800** |
| 25th | Car Note | $321.30 |
| 30th | Major Credit Card | $185 |
| Total Bills Week 5: | | $2056.30 |

| | |
|---|---|
| Total in Checking: | $2360.30 |
| Week 5 Bills: | -$2056.30 |
| **New Checking Balance/Flow #:** | **$250.00** |

## *Building A Debt-Free Plan*

On the week-five plan, there will be an extra $300 in income. I recommend that $300 be applied to building your $1000 emergency fund, if that has not been completed. However, if you have your $1000 emergency fund in place, I recommend you apply the $300 to your smallest debt, which in the example above would be the Major Credit Card bill. Again, be sure to notice the plan started with **$250** and ended with **$250. You know where your money is going.**

# Chapter 7

## Let It Flow- The Secret to Having Enough Money

**A Debt-Free Tip: Start your plan with a certain amount of money each month and end with the same amount of money.**

**"The Lord said, 'If as one people speaking the same language they have begun to do this, then nothing they plan to do will be impossible for them.'" Genesis 11:6 (New International Version)**

As I mentioned, when we were more than fifty thousand dollars in debt--not including our house note--our family struggled with the common financial problem of not enough money to cover our monthly bill commitments.

You want to get out of debt and stay out of debt. And you know you need a financial plan, but you find it tough to stick to, right? Often, there just does not seem to be enough money to budget, and people throw money at bills without a plan. (You know: that stack of bills on the kitchen counter.)

With the paycheck spent, here come the credit cards, and another dose of stress over money. I see this frequently with clients.

Let me help you get out of that dreaded trap with a simple program I devised to live Debt-Free–a program that uses a different type of budgeting, one that actually works for busy families who are stretching to make ends meet.

## *The Flow Number*

Instead of going with the flow when it comes to your money, I want to teach you how to use Kelly's Cash Flow System using my "flow number plan" to have enough money to cover your bills each month. The "flow number" in Kelly's CA$H Flow System is the key to getting out of debt and staying out of debt. It is the amount you start your budget with and it will be the amount you end with at the end of the month.

An example is you start with $500, pay all bills and expenses, and end with $500. By doing this it teaches you to name what every dollar in your paycheck is for (food, electric bill, savings, etc.).

**How did I discover this technique?**

I discovered this technique from observing everyday people and how they spend money. I had clients, for example, who would come to me and say, "Kelly, at the end of the month we had $500, so we went to the water park." What the clients did not realize was that they needed $300 of the $500 to carry them through the next month until their paycheck arrived.

Since the clients spent $500 at the water park, by the second week of the following month they had no money for groceries and did not get paid until Friday, so they felt forced to use a credit card. This approach, of course, leads to growing debt. When you are in this situation, you are back to what I sadly call

101

"the rat in a wheel." Here is how you live: Running and running, exhausted with your finances, not getting anywhere and unsure how to get out of this trap. The "flow number" system will get you out of the trap and help relieve the financial pressure you feel. You will identify the weeks when your paycheck is not enough to cover that week's bills and how to plan to cover the shortfall by using your flow number.

The flow number will help you manage the money you have coming in with the expenses that are going out. It does not take a rocket scientist to know that the money coming in has to match the money going out for expenses. If you are in the situation where you have more expenses than income, then there are only two options to fix that problem:

Option 1 is to cut your expenses to match your income, which may mean reducing your cable or cell phone package.

Option 2 is to bring in more income by either selling something to pay off debt or by getting a second job to meet your financial obligations.

Numbers on paper show you where you are financially and you must see it for what it is, not for what you want it to be. The biggest secret to doing a successful budget is figuring out exactly what your flow number is--the amount of money you need at the end of one month to have enough cash to carry you through the next month. The flow number, unique to you and your finances, is a critical part of making your budget work and can be learned, no matter how much you hate math!

Most people try to do budgets based on a calendar month, from the first through the thirtieth or thirty-first. Budgets done this way, never work.

Instead, start with the dates you get paid each month and the due dates of your bills. Get a notebook or a tablet or a computer spread sheet—whatever works for you. This will be your money plan, and you will determine how the money will flow.

Jump into this process *before* the month begins.

Next you will need to learn to figure *how* each dollar will be spent and *when* each dollar will be spent, including utility bills, groceries, car note, and so forth.

**It is important to have a plan for every dollar so later you do not have to ask yourself the question, "Where did all of my money go?"**

Everyone's flow number is different because we each have different incomes, different bills, and different payment due dates. If most of your bills are due at the beginning of the month, you will have a higher flow number. If your bills are spread out during the month, then you will have a smaller flow number. The examples I offer here can show you how this works, and you can use the information for your specific circumstances.

**Figuring Your Flow Number**

In order to determine your flow number, you'll need to figure out during which weeks you have less income and more bills. Use this simple formula for each week:

Weekly income minus bills due this week equals _____,

Example 1:

Week 1 Income of $750 – week 1 bills of $1000 =      - $250

Week 2 Income of $1650 – week 2 bills of $1480.60 =   + $169.40

Week 3 Income of $750 – week 3 bills of $607.40 =    + $142.60

Week 4 Income of $1850 – week 4 bills of $1912.00 =   - $62.00

The highest negative number is the flow number. In the example above, $250 works as the flow number. The flow number in this example can be more than $250, but it can never be less than $250. If it is more than $250, it will give more of a cushion in the checking account. If the flow number is less than $250, then at some point this person will be in the negative.

Always stay in the positive in your checking account. If your checking account goes below zero balance you will trigger excessive bank fees. If your checking account is at zero, you are not in the negative but obviously *very* close. If more money makes you more comfortable, you may want to set your flow number higher.  For example, the family above might want to set their flow number at $350 instead of $250 to allow an extra $100 cushion.

The great thing about the flow number is that it is the number you start with each month, and it is the number you will end with each month if you plan for every dollar you bring home.  Your flow number can be any number you want as long as it is not less than the highest negative number in the budget.

The flow number for the example below is $450.  This is another example showing you how to determine your flow number:

Amount paid each week:

Week 1 $500

Week 2 $500

Week 3 $500

Week 4 $500

Monthly Total:  $2000


Now that we have our income we want to break our income down weekly according to our bills.

### Week 1 – Paid $500

| | |
|---|---|
| Grocery | $100 |
| Fuel | $25 |
| Me Money | $25 |
| Rent | $500 |
| Donation | $200 |
| **Total Bills:** | **$850** |
| **Week 1 Short** | -$350 |

### Week 2 – Paid $500

| | |
|---|---|
| Grocery | $100 |
| Fuel | $25 |
| Me Money | $25 |
| Truck Note | $350 |
| Electricity | $100 |
| **Total Bills:** | **$600** |
| **Week 2 Short** | -$100 |

### Week 3 – Paid $500

| | |
|---|---|
| Grocery | $100 |
| Fuel | $25 |
| Me Money | $25 |
| Savings Deposit | $150 |
| **Total Bills:** | **$300** |
| **Week 3 Over** | +$200 |

### Week 4 – Paid $500

| | |
|---|---|
| Grocery | $100 |
| Fuel | $25 |
| Me Money | $25 |
| Water | $50 |
| Cable | $50 |
| **Total Bills:** | **$250** |
| **Week 4 Over** | +$250 |

# The Flow Number

**What determines the Flow Number?**

| | |
|---|---|
| **Week 1** | **Short -$350** |
| **Week 2** | **Short -$100** |
| **Week 3** | **Over $200** |
| **Week 4** | **Over $250** |

**Your <u>Total</u> <u>Shortage</u> for the Month = _$450_**

## <u>Stay in the BLACK by using the Flow Number</u>

| | <u>Week 1</u> | <u>Week 2</u> | <u>Week 3</u> | <u>Week 4</u> |
|---|---|---|---|---|
| _Flow #_ | _$450_ | _$100_ | _$0_ | _$200_ |
| **Income** | <u>$500</u> | <u>$500</u> | <u>$500</u> | <u>$500</u> |
| **Total:** | $950 | $600 | $500 | $700 |
| -Bills | <u>$-850</u> | <u>$-600</u> | <u>$-300</u> | <u>$-250</u> |
| = | $100 | $0 | $200 | _$450 Flow #_ |

You can visibly see that using $450 as your flow number will keep you from going negative in your checking account and will avoid NSF fees.

## Don't go in the RED by not using the Flow Number

| | Week 1 | Week 2 | Week 3 | Week 4 |
|---|---|---|---|---|
| *Flow #* | *$0* | $-350 | $-450 | $-250 |
| **Income** | **$500** | **$500** | **$500** | **$500** |
| **Total:** | **$500** | **$150** | **$50** | **$250** |
| -Bills | $-850 | $-600 | $-300 | $-250 |
| = | $-350 | $-450 | $-250 | *$0 Flow #* |

You can visibly see here that if you just start with your income and don't have a flow number that you will go negative in your checking account and will be charged a fee for the insufficient funds. The flow number is the heartbeat of the budget. View the line chart provided on the next page to get a better picture of how critical the flow number is to the budget.

## Flow Number:  The Heartbeat of the Budget

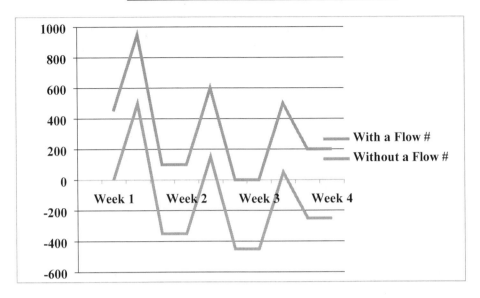

One key to living Debt-Free and having enough money each month, is determining what your flow number is.  This is how much cash you need in the checking account at the end of one month to flow you through until the following month.

*What is the flow number for your family?*

You may feel overwhelmed as you start on your flow number, but you can do it.  As you decide to live Debt-Free, you will probably have to make changes in your spending and make tough choices.  But hundreds of people have told me how this approach has changed their lives.

Consider these entries from a client's journal (used with her permission):

"I have *never* saved money before in my life, but now I am! I have been thinking about all that you have said. I decided to write my testimonial today because I realized today that I truly will be able to do this program. I went shopping with my sister today, and I was able to leave both stores without purchasing a single thing.

Now don't get me wrong; I picked up several things and actually carried them around with me, but then I could hear your sweet voice in the back of my mind and knew that you would not want me spending my 'flow number' that I have to have to get through the next month on a $40 pair of flip flops. I realized that the flip flops were a want and not a need. I thought about the *consequences of my spending* for the first time today!

I could have potentially ruined what you worked so hard putting together for me, and what I worked so hard to pay for, by spending all of my money. I left the store empty handed but feeling *very* liberated that I finally said *No*. I guess I will always be a 'recovering shopaholic.'

And then her follow-up:

"Update: I was so excited when I paid all of my bills, put money in savings and filled my envelopes. I am so much more aware of how much I am spending now. My little boy wanted Burger King after church last night and asked if there was any money in the envelope? I told him, 'No, we have food at home.' I just wanted to let you know that I have really found it a lot easier than I thought it would be."

This client felt such freedom by living Debt-Free that she referred her sister to me—and they gave their mother my one-on-one financial coaching services as a gift. The women have taken action to change their family tree, a gift that has literally kept on giving throughout their family.

# Chapter 8

## How to Pay Cash for a Car: The Best Kept Financial Success Secret

## A Debt-Free Tip: Pay yourself $417 per month.

**"He who puts up security for another will surely suffer, but whoever refuses to strike hands in pledge is safe."**

**Proverbs 11:15 (New International Version)**

You are probably thinking the same thing I thought several years ago: "Paying cash for a car will never be possible for me." We often think of a car note as something we will always have, but it does not have to be that way. Cars are built to last these days and should, for financial benefits, be kept for at least ten years or a minimum of 200,000 miles. We are spoiled and tend to want to buy a new car as soon as we finish paying for the current one.

**New cars are not an investment.**

Vehicles depreciate twenty to thirty percent immediately and go down in value like a rock falling to the earth from the sky.

To make it clearer: If you buy a $25,000 vehicle, drive around the block and pull back into the dealership, the vehicle is now only worth $17,500.

That new car smell is very expensive.

## *Pay Cash for a Car*

What if I asked you to invest $500 per month with me for forty eight months? That would come to $24,000 in four years. If at the end of four years I told you your investment was worth only $7,500, would you be happy or upset?

New cars depreciate seventy percent in the first four years. Do not be drawn into thinking of cars as investments, unless you own a car dealership. A vehicle is to get us from point A to point B safely. In today's world, we spend money we don't have to purchase cars we can't afford to impress people we don't even know or like. Do not allow pride to get in the way.

Only purchase a vehicle you can afford, one that will not put you in financial hardship. Most people who drive prestige cars are not millionaires, although their vehicles lead people to believe otherwise. In a survey, *The Wall Street Journal* found that thirty-five percent of people believed to qualify as "rich," a person must drive a car that costs $75,000 or more. Millionaires know better. The average millionaire spends less than $32,000 on a vehicle.

That means that, according to public opinion, more than ninety percent of wealthy people would be perceived as poorer than they are. These people do not put their hard-earned money into objects that go down in value.

How about you? Don't you work too hard for your money to use it on something that loses value?

**The Secret to Buying a Car with Cash**

I am often asked, "What is the secret to paying cash for a car?" The answer: patience and discipline. In only *six* years you can pay $20,000 cash for a vehicle, using this approach:

- Purchase a car for $2,000 cash.

- Drive the $2,000 car for *two* years while putting $417 per month in savings. By doing this you will earn interest instead of paying interest to someone else. In just two years, you will have more than $10,000 to buy another car.

- Sell the $2,000 car.

- Purchase a car for $10,000 cash. In two years you have moved up from a $2,000 car to a $10,000 car – not bad.

- Drive the $10,000 car for *four* years while putting $417 per month in savings. In four years you will have $20,000 to pay cash for another car.

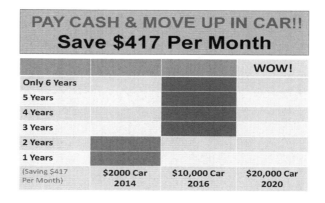

## *Pay Cash for a Car*

Do not let your car drive you into poverty. Another tip is never co-sign on a vehicle for anyone. If the dealership is requiring a co-signer on the loan, it is because they already know that the borrower cannot afford to make the payments. If you do choose to co-sign, be ready to take full responsibility for the loan.

If you feel you must finance a vehicle, I recommend that it be for two to three years or less. If you have to borrow money for a vehicle for more than three years, you cannot afford the vehicle. **Again:** *If you have to pay a car note for longer than three years, you cannot afford that vehicle. And paying cash is always preferable.*


**Other costs to consider**

The purchase of a vehicle brings other expenses, including auto insurance, fuel, and vehicle maintenance. These must be factored into your spending plan. Being a savvy car buyer requires doing your homework and reviewing options. It will vary according to the dealer and, if you borrow money, the loan company.

Sometimes paying cash does not get you the best price. Finance companies offer rebates to entice you to finance with them, earning them money through interest rates. A buyer might finance a car, get the benefit of a financing rebate and pay the car off in full before the first payment is due. In most cases, you can get full benefit of the rebate and still write a smaller check for the car.

One more note: Dealers often tell buyers they must make the first three payments if they intend to take advantage of a rebate. Dealers are usually paid a flat fee of a couple of hundred dollars. That flat fee is charged back to them if the consumer pays off the car before three payments are made, but by law, you can pay it off at any time.

Paying cash is *always* best if you want to live Debt-Free. Instead of paying interest on a car loan, you can earn interest on the money you save each month to buy your car. Paying cash is a plus for both the dealership and you. Paying cash often allows you to negotiate a good price and removes financial risks for the dealership or lien holder.

I will never forget something my new father-in-law said to me at our wedding reception: "The secret to being financially successful is to live life without a car note."

I didn't put much thought into it because my husband and I each had a car note. As time passed, I have come to realize he was right.

Discipline is making the choice between what you want now and what you want most. Not having a car note brings more financial freedom to your life. Not having a car note helps drive you toward living a Debt-Free & Wealthy life.

# Pay Cash for a Car

## A Car-Savings-Plan for your Child

One of the challenges of parenthood and grandparenthood is deciding when and if to buy your children or grandchildren a car. Cars are expensive, as we've discussed. I watched all three of money expert Dave Ramsey's children successfully work this plan. You can start this plan at any time with your children.

## How It Works

When our daughter turned ten, we sat down with her and talked about saving for a car. We told her we would not buy her a car when she was older but were starting a 401K Car Plan.

The plan works like this. Any money she earns and wants to put in the 401K car fund, we match dollar for dollar. So if she earns twenty dollars and wants to put ten dollars in the car fund, we match it with ten dollars. She then will have twenty dollars being deposited into the car fund. We remind her that the amount she saves will affect the type of car she will be able to afford. Will she purchase a car or a bicycle? Only hard work and time will tell.

We call it the "401K Car Plan" to get her used to the term "401K," a retirement savings plan. Of course, as a teenager, she does not understand precisely what the term 401K means. However, over time she is becoming familiar with the concept. When she gets out in the working world and employers ask her if she wants to participate in the 401K Plan, she will know this refers to saving money and a match of money.

Through this program, she is learning it is possible to save and pay cash for big purchases. Another perk is that working long and hard to pay cash for a car increases the likelihood that she will take better care of the vehicle and perhaps even drive safer. (We hope and pray she drives safely.)

We record all entries on a yellow pad: Date, her deposit, match, total deposit, and total balance. She actually is the one to write it down and gets excited about watching the growth of the car fund. She is required to help with certain chores at home without getting paid, what we consider part of her family responsibilities. We each have chores to keep the household running smoothly and she is no different. She does not get paid to make her bed every day before school, for example. She does not get paid to empty the dishwasher or fold clothes.

Occasionally, she earns money for taking on a special household assignment such as cleaning up the yard, washing our cars, or watering plants. Other car fund deposits have come from birthdays, Christmas and from her grandparents for a good report card. (While her dad and I are always pleased with good grades, we do not pay her for those, believing we must teach her to do her best and to know we have confidence in her to do so.)

This fund is helping our daughter learn about saving, investing and even building money for retirement. If you do everything for your children, you are not helping them; you are enabling and hurting them. Chores and responsibilities help them learn how to become responsible, successful adults. As parents, it is our job to teach children responsibility and how to do for themselves—preparing them for the time when they will fly away from the nest.

**Chapter 9**

**Learning to Pay Off Student Loans**

**A Debt-Free Tip:  Student Loans are almost impossible to discharge in bankruptcy.**

**"The wicked borrows and does not pay back, but the righteous is gracious and gives." Psalms 37:21 (New American Standard Version)**

The phone call went like this:

"Kelly, I am so overwhelmed, stressed and worried about my family. The weight of this debt is so heavy that I cannot continue to carry it anymore. I think we just need to file for bankruptcy."

This type of call, unfortunately, is not uncommon in my business. I have had the same call from clients in their thirties, forties, fifties, and even sixties. I set up an appointment with these clients to help lead them to a Debt-Free life. As the couple entered my office, the distress in their eyes and the heaviness on their hearts were obvious. The clients, in their forties, had $115,000 in debt, with only $15,000 of that as credit card debt. The remaining $100,000 was student loan debt. Thank goodness they called because I was able to address something many people do not realize:  Student loans are almost impossible to have discharged in bankruptcy. They would have filed bankruptcy on only $15,000 in credit card debt. It is important to realize, as long as they are breathing, they will have to pay back the student loans.

Filing bankruptcy would not help their situation.

I wish there were a mandatory class to teach all students exactly how student loans work *before* they could actually receive a student loan. It is crucial for them to understand that this borrowed money is not free. While a college education is an important step for many people and can help increase earning power, it requires—you guessed it—financial planning.

Before you borrow for student loans, do some soul searching to figure out what your passion is and what type of work you will enjoy. Ask someone in the field you are interested in if you can shadow them for a few days to see exactly what the day-to-day job involves. Unfortunately, I have seen many students graduate with degrees in different fields than the one they are working in and faced with paying for an education that is not being used as planned. Apply for grants that do not have to be paid back. Do not take borrowing money lightly because the cost is very high.

According to America Student Assistance, a nonprofit organization that helps families manage student debt, sixty percent of the twenty million students who attend college each year take out a student loan. There is between $902 billion and $1 trillion in total outstanding student loan debt today. My opinion is that this will be the next bubble to burst in our economy. Nearly thirty percent of college students who take out a student loan never actually graduate. Two out of five student loan borrowers–or forty-one percent –are delinquent at some point in the first five years after entering a repayment plan.

Clearly, young adults are struggling with paying student loan debt. If you decide to take out a student loan, borrow the minimum amount needed for school, *not* the maximum amount they allow you to borrow.

I have seen so many young adults make the mistake of borrowing the maximum so they can use the money for purchases other than for school. Some borrow more money so they can move out of the dormitory and get an apartment. I have seen them borrow more money to buy a new vehicle. When you are in college, you should not borrow money to live a higher lifestyle. It will come back to hurt you later. Work and pay cash for college if possible. If you choose to borrow, borrow the minimum amount needed.

Another important thing to understand about student loans is that while the student loans are deferred, interest continues to accrue. You may have a break from making payments for a year, but that loan is growing every day. Start paying on your student loans as soon as possible and continue until they are paid off. Regardless of your age or income, you are required to pay on that loan until it is gone.

# *Student Loans*

If you choose not to pay, the federal government can take up to twenty-five percent of your wages with no notice. This process is known as garnishing your pay. It means that one day you could receive your paycheck and it can be twenty-five percent less than you usually receive.

If you owe taxes or student loans, I recommend you get them paid off as soon as possible because the U.S. government does not play around when it comes to collecting individual debts. A scholarship or grant does not have to be paid back, but a student loan does, with interest. With a plan, paying back a student loan is doable. I've been delighted to watch many clients do so.

One hard-working single mom with $80,000 in student loan debt came to me at a loss about how to handle Sallie Mae, the federal student loan program. Together we contacted Sallie Mae and got her loans out of deferment and onto a payment plan that worked for her.

"I felt very overwhelmed and did not know where to turn," she says. "I had $80,000 in student loan debt and felt as if I could not breathe. The Debt-Free with Kelly program started me on a life altering path in November 2012. As a single mom, I can't express enough how much this program has changed my life for the better, and I am proud to say that today, less than two years later, I do not live life in financial stress and fear."

– Ulrica – 2012

As college costs increase, so will the level of student loan debt in the United States.

**A few things to consider**

** Don't be naïve about how student loans work.

** Avoid private student loans offered by banks; they usually have higher interest rates.

** If you decide to get a student loan, keep a record of how much you borrow each semester.

**Ask what the estimated note will be on the total amount you have borrowed and how many years it will take to pay off the loan. The answer to these questions help you prepare for the payments you will have to make after graduation.

** When you decide to go to college, research costs as part of your college choice. In-state tuition is cheaper than out-of-state tuition. Also, research the career path you are interested in. Find out how much that job pays and if it is in demand.

** As you consider your field of study, learn about possible jobs, and the hours you are required to work. Do you have to work weekends? Do jobs in this field offer benefits? Will you be required to relocate and how often?

# *Student Loans*

** Do not assume that just because you have a diploma that you will automatically start work at $50,000 per year.

## Doing Work You Love

Many people work not only to earn a living but to make a difference in the world. Having a good job that fulfills you and helps pay the bills is a blessing.

We never know what the next day holds for us. At the age of twenty-five, a gentleman had what could have been a life altering experience. With a wife, a three-year-old daughter and an infant son at home, he worked long hours to support his family. While sitting at a red light in New Orleans, he sneezed and lost his eye sight. Cars started honking, so he knew the light must have turned green so he slowly drove the car to the side of the road, feeling for the curb. He opened the door and, before long an officer walked up and identified himself asking what was wrong. The gentleman explained what had happened and the officer drove him to the hospital.

After four days in the hospital, *my father's* eyesight returned. My family's life could have been forever altered that day, but thankfully, God had other plans for all of us. When someone says "God bless you" to my father when he sneezes, it has strong personal meaning. Do not take life for granted. Discover your purpose and serve others.

If you can figure out what you are passionate about and learn to make money doing it, you will enjoy your work—and life—more. This is the best gift to yourself and to others because you will be right where God wants you: serving others with enthusiasm.

Some people discover this passion at a young age and some later in life. It took a journey to get me to this work I love. I was 38-years-old before I figured out what God was calling me to do -- to work on money plans for families and help others learn to live Debt-Free & Wealthy.

Take time to reflect on the work you are meant to do, the work that uses the special talents you have been given. You do not want to spend the precious time you have on earth doing work that is a grind, boring or not helpful to others.

# Chapter 10

## Saving, Investing, and Retirement...It *Is* Closer Than You Think

**A Debt-Free Tip: If you learn to save money, one day it will return the favor. It will be there for you when you need it.**

**"The rich rule over the poor and the borrower becomes the lender's slave." Proverbs 22:7 (New American Standard Version)**

Sooner rather than later.

That is when retirement will be here for you.

As soon as you are Debt-Free except for your house payment, get busy saving. Save, save and save some more. Decide how to invest your savings. I cannot stress enough how important this piece of the puzzle is. When you are young, you feel that retirement is so far away that you will worry about it later. The problem is *later* may show up too late.

Ironically, time is your best friend when it comes to planning for retirement. The earlier and younger you start investing, the better off you will be. You cannot start too early. My 15-year-old daughter works during the summer and we have taught her to put 20 percent of what she brings home in a Roth IRA. She is saving early for retirement and in a Roth IRA the money will grow tax free and she can withdraw her contributions at any time tax free and

127

penalty free. She gives 10 percent to the church and uses the remaining 70 percent for herself.

She understands that this means #wealthyoneday in her language. This has helped her have a better understanding of the stock market and how a Roth IRA works. It builds her self-esteem and she is excited to watch it grow from month to month. As parents, it is our job to teach our children how to work and save.

**Where do you start?**

Once you are debt-free except your home and have a fully funded emergency fund of six months of expenses, consider two options.

Option one is to keep your savings in a money market account where it is safe and will earn a little more interest than a regular savings account. By putting the emergency fund here, the funds are liquid and easily accessible for when that emergency does happen. (Yes, an emergency is going to happen, I can guarantee it.)

Option two is to put half of the fully-funded emergency fund in the money market or savings account and the other half in a ***Roth IRA***. This will enable you to have funds in the market, which should earn more than a savings account or money market account. However, it also has a higher risk because it is in the market.

The investment of money is a serious and often complicated process, which carries varying degrees of risk. I encourage you to develop a relationship with a financial professional to advise you. As we've discussed, each person's finances are different, and personal advice from a trusted investment broker, financial planner, banker, or a CPA can help. The investment information here is intended to give you an idea of approaches you might consider but should not be your sole guide to investing.

Do not let fear or uncertainty keep you from saving and investing for your future. Educate yourself about investments. Seek the help of reliable, trustworthy investment professionals. Be sure the investment professional fully explains your investments to you and that you are comfortable with your advisor. You should never invest money in anything that you do not understand yourself.

There are two types of IRAs (Individual Retirement Accounts), a Traditional IRA, invested with pre-tax dollars, and a Roth IRA that is invested with after-tax dollars.

I love the Roth IRA. A Roth IRA grows tax–free, and when you withdraw it at 59 ½ or after, you withdraw it tax-free. However, the sweet thing about the Roth IRA is you can withdraw any contributions made to the Roth IRA at any time with *no* penalty. The current contribution to a Roth IRA if you are under the age of 50 years of age is $5500, and if you are 50 years old or older, the maximum contribution is $6500. These amounts change from year to year so be sure to check with a professional to get the current maximum contribution amounts.

If a big emergency happens and you need the second half of your emergency fund, you will be able to get that money in about two to ten days and pay no taxes or penalties. If you convert money from a Traditional IRA to a Roth IRA, however, that money cannot be withdrawn from the Roth tax-free and penalty-free for at least five years. Only the after-tax dollars deposited into a Roth IRA can be withdrawn at any time with no penalty, not the conversion dollars before five years.

Example: If your emergency fund of six months of expenses is $30,000, then you could put $15,000 in a money market account or savings account and invest the other $15,000 in a Roth IRA. If you are not able to invest in the Roth IRA because you make too much money, then you probably will want to keep the full $30,000 in a money market account or savings account. Your emergency fund needs to be quickly accessible without penalties or fees so do not put it in a CD (Certificate of Deposit).

# Savings, Investment & Retirement

The best part about the stock market is that if you use the standard diversification to diversify your funds and invest for the long haul, you are almost certain to make money as history has proven. Ecclesiastes 11:1-6 talks about this.

Standard diversification consists of the following:

- 25% Growth & Income (Large Cap funds – Large Companies)
- 25% Growth (Mid Cap funds – Medium Size Companies)
- 25% Aggressive Growth (Small Cap funds – Small Companies)
- 25% International (Foreign or Global Funds)

If you invest in the market and diversify this way over a five-year period, based on previous market performance, you will make money ninety-seven percent of the time. If you invest in the market and diversify over a ten-year period, based on previous market performance, you will make money one-hundred percent of the time.

To help you have a better understanding of investing in the market, consider the following:

If you place $100,000 in a box under your bed and pull it out in ten years from now you will still have $100,000 in the box, and that is only if you didn't spend any of the money.

If you invest $100,000 over a ten year period and it averages a 9% rate of return, then in 10 years you would then have $190,000. This is based only on simple interest, not compound interest which will give you even greater growth.

If you invest $100,000 over a ten-year period and it averages only a 5% rate of return, then in 10 years you would have $150,000. Again, this is based only on simple interest, not compound interest which will give you greater growth.

**Planning for Retirement**

After you have your three-to-six-month emergency fund in place, the second step is to invest fifteen percent into a retirement account. You will likely want to invest into a 401K, and a Roth IRA. (If your income is too high for the Roth, invest in the Traditional IRA instead.)

I recommend you invest up to the company match in your 401K, because that is free money. *And who doesn't like free money?* Consider investing the rest into a Roth IRA, and once it is funded to the maximum contribution allowed based on your age, you can put the rest into a mutual fund.

Entire books are written about investments, and I will not attempt to cover them all here. However, let me emphasize the importance of deciding what type of investment accounts are right for you. These are tools that can help you as you learn to save and build wealth through your Debt-Free with Kelly

journey. I like to use mutual funds, Traditional IRAs, and Roth IRAs. It is okay

to have a 500 Index mutual fund and a 500 Index Traditional IRA and a 500

Index Roth IRA if you really like that fund or you can have each in a different

type of fund. I do not recommend single stocks because they carry a high degree

of risks. For more information on investing, I suggest you visit with your

financial advisor or contact an investment professional.

When selecting a fund, you should look for certain things:

**Make sure the fund's expense ratio is less than one percent. If it is

higher than one percent, they are charging too much for that fund and keeping

too much of your money.

**Check the fund inception date to be sure the fund has been open for at

least ten years. If the fund has not been open ten years, it does not have the track

record needed to determine if it is a good fund to invest in or not.

**Compare the rate of return since the inception date, which is simply

the date the fund opened. This will protect you and help you make the best

choice for your family when investing.

The investing chart on the next page shows *some* funds from The

Vanguard Group, Inc. as of 12/31/13. Understand that some years the funds will

perform higher and some years the funds will perform lower.

The year 2013 was a great year. Highlighted are the funds with a low expense ratio, funds that have been open for at least ten years and funds with the best rate of return since inception. Notice that the funds for this company are divided into the four diversification recommendations.

### Vanguard Funds

| Fund | Asset Class | Exp. Ratio | 1 yr | 3yr | 5yr | 10 yr | % Since Inception | Inception Date |
|---|---|---|---|---|---|---|---|---|
| Equity Income | Large | 0.31 | 20.60 | 24.66 | 9.97 | 9.20 | 10.18 | 03/21/1988 |
| High Div. Yield Index | Large | 0.20 | 30.13 | 17.37 | 16.72 | ---- | 6.11 | 11/16/2006 |
| Windsor | Large | 0.41 | 36.08 | 16.42 | 19.53 | 7.04 | 11.58 | 10/23/1958 |
| 500 Index | Large | 0.17 | 32.18 | 16.00 | 17.81 | 7.29 | 11.04 | 08/31/1976 |
| Total Stock Mrk Index | Large | 0.17 | 33.35 | 16.11 | 18.72 | 7.99 | 9.49 | 04/27/1992 |
| Mid-Cap Value Index | Mid | 0.24 | 37.42 | 16.61 | 21.56 | ---- | 8.38 | 08/24/2006 |
| Extended Mrk Index | Mid | 0.28 | 38.19 | 16.32 | 22.47 | 10.17 | 11.24 | 12/21/1987 |
| Mid-Cap Growth | Mid | 0.54 | 34.15 | 15.94 | 21.72 | 9.75 | 10.65 | 12/31/1997 |
| Small-Cap Index | Small | 0.30 | 37.62 | 16.45 | 22.38 | 10.20 | 10.87 | 10/03/1960 |
| Explorer | Small | 0.51 | 44.36 | 17.62 | 23.08 | 9.20 | 9.43 | 12/11/1967 |
| Sm-Cap Growth Index | Small | 0.24 | 37.98 | 16.86 | 24.23 | 10.63 | 8.96 | 05/21/1998 |
| International Exp. | Foreign | 0.43 | 30.24 | 7.22 | 17.32 | 9.95 | 10.31 | 11/04/1996 |
| International Growth | Foreign | 0.48 | 22.95 | 8.40 | 15.84 | 8.66 | 11.15 | 09/30/1981 |
| Pacific Stock Index | Foreign | 0.26 | 17.36 | 5.24 | 10.34 | 6.26 | 2.28 | 06/18/1990 |

## Savings, Investment & Retirement

This chart is used only as a basic tool to teach you what to look for in funds and how to make a selection. Again, this is just to give you an idea of how it works. I am not a licensed broker and recommend you consult an investment professional for further details and education on investments.

*Your financial future is in your hands; don't let it slip by you. No one is going to take better care of you than you. The responsibility is yours to make the right financial choices for your financial future today.*

I beg you to not be like the client who came to me at the age of sixty-two with only $45,000 saved for retirement. This client was ashamed and embarrassed, but worst of all, out of time. He still owed $75,000 on his home, plus owed a $78,000 home equity line of credit, $5,000 on a car, $2,000 in medical debt, and $70,000 in credit card debt. He was $2,200 short per month on income to meet the minimum payments on everything.

Ten years earlier he was living life to the fullest and trying to keep up with the Joneses and this is where it got him: broke at the age of sixty-two. He did not get in this situation overnight and he was not going to get out of it overnight. By reducing his lifestyle, selling some things and getting an extra job on the weekends, he could get out of debt. When getting out of debt, you have to be willing to sacrifice some things to win financially.

Money is very real. It can help you but if you do not respect it, it can hurt you. Saving for retirement takes "time and money" so when you do retire you will have "time and money."

## Term Life Insurance & A Will

Along with being on the same page it is important to take care of each other by having sufficient life insurance and a will in place. I recommend term life insurance only. It is inexpensive, sufficient and the rate never increases during the term of the policy regardless of any health issues that may come up through the years. I suggest ten times your income or at least a minimum of enough to pay off all of your debt, including the home and to cover the cost of a funeral. It is important to get the policy for a term that will carry you until retirement age. At that time you become what we call "self-insured."

If you are debt free and your home is paid for, drawing social security and you have $500,000 in mutual funds and retirement accounts, you no longer need life insurance. If something happens to you, there should be plenty of money for a funeral and plenty of money remaining to take care of your family. Remember, you are not purchasing life insurance for yourself; you are purchasing life insurance to protect the loved ones that will be left behind.

Do you have a will?  Get one!  You can go to www.uslegalforms.com to do this or to your attorney.  Do not die without a will.  This is part of your responsibility of taking care of the family.  A will is to ensure that the wishes of the deceased are carried out and it can save the family from having to go through succession and help avoid family disputes.  I also recommend that you get a Living Will.  This will legally express your wishes should you become terminally ill or unable to speak for yourself.  This will also state who you would put in charge should a final decision have to be made.

Another important thing you need to know about a will is that **all** wills are state specific.  If you live in Alabama and move to the great state of Louisiana, you will need a Louisiana Will and the Alabama Will is no longer valid.  Understand that if you move a year later to California, the Louisiana Will is not worth the paper it is written on.  Again, all wills are state specific.  Please, if you do not have a will, get one today.


**Social Security**

If you are age fifty or older, make an appointment at your Social Security Administration office and obtain an estimate of the benefits you will be able to draw at retirement age.  You need to know how much you can draw at age sixty-two and how much can you draw at sixty-seven. *Brace yourself because it is not going to be as much as you think it is.*

Visiting with the local office, plus your financial advisor, is helpful because Social Security payments vary according to age, number of quarters you paid into the system, and a variety of other factors. In addition, if you are married, your spouse's payments can affect your decisions about when to draw Social Security. However, generally you should wait until age seventy to draw Social Security benefits if you can. If that is not possible, wait until age sixty-six or sixty-seven. These are the reasons why:

- From ages 66 to 67, your benefits increase 6% per year.
- From ages 67 to 70, your benefits increase 8% per year.

It is to your benefit financially to postpone drawing Social Security until you have to take it.

**Another way to get the eight-percent increase:**

If a husband earns more than his wife (and has been paying into Social Security), he will receive more Social Security per month. At age sixty-seven, he can claim Social Security, then suspend it. This allows his Social Security benefits to increase over the next three years at the eight-percent rate and he can take it at age seventy.

# Savings, Investment & Retirement

If he claims it and suspends it, his wife can claim a spousal benefit, which is fifty percent of his Social Security. At age seventy, he collects full Social Security benefits and his wife will take one-hundred percent of her own benefits, if they are more than half of his, but not both.

**You cannot draw a pension *and* full Social Security unless you have paid in thirty years of service to the Social Security system. Usually, you can only draw one or the other, but not both.** An example would be working as a welder for 28 years, then working as a sheriff's deputy for 15 years, you would draw the pension from the sheriff's deputy job and only a percentage from the Social Security system from when you worked as a welder. Make an appointment with your Social Security office to review your individual situation.

In order to draw off of her husband, the wife's maximum payable has to be less than half of his maximum payable. If the husband dies, his wife's Social Security will go up to the max of what he was receiving.

The following example will help determine the difference in drawing at age sixty-two and sixty-seven:

Age 62 draw $883

Age 67 draw $1254.30

The difference is $371 more per month.

$883 X 12 months = $10,596 per year x 5 years = $52,980

$371 X 12 months = $ 4,452 per year

$52,980 / $4,452 = 11.90 years; 12 years to make up that money

67 + 12 years = 79 years old; you have to decide if it would be worth it. You may decide that it is best to draw at age 62 when you are younger and can enjoy it. You may feel like you may not live until age seventy-nine.

I had another client who was sixty years old with $400,000 in retirement, looking forward to retiring soon due to health issues. However, this client owed $55,000 on his home, had $28,000 in car debt, and his monthly expenses were$5,000 per month with no extra income to apply to the debt. Social Security would pay him $2,000 per month, so he would have to draw $3,000 from his retirement each month to maintain his current lifestyle.

If he pulls $3,000 per month from his retirement ($36,000 per year) his retirement of $400,000 will only last eleven years and a month. At that time he will only be seventy-three years old and out of money.

That shows that $400,000 saved for retirement may not be as much as you think it is. Debt has to be paid off, and lifestyle has to be cut in order for those numbers to work.

**I will keep saying this:** *How much money you have saved determines at what age you will be able to retire!*

# Chapter 11

## Understanding Long Term Care & Medicare

**A Debt-Free Tip:  Understand your plan if you choose not to get Long Term Care.**

**"Know also that wisdom is sweet to your soul; if you find it, there is a future hope for you, and your hope will not be cut off."**

**Proverbs 24:14 (New International Version)**

Long term care is an insurance that you should consider purchasing in your late fifties and early sixties.  It is very important that this part of your journey is not ignored.  According to the American Association of Home and Services for the Aging, sixty-nine percent of us will need some form of long-term care after the age of sixty-five.  If you become ill, the wealth you have spent a lifetime building will not end up going to your care if you have Long-Term Care Insurance.

Not having LTC insurance can be a $300,000 to $400,000 mistake.

The average stay in some sort of facility for care is 2 years, 8 months. One in ninety-six will use their home insurance for a fire.  One in five will use their car insurance due to some sort of car accident, but two out of three people will use their LTC policy. Premiums for women are higher than premiums for men because women live longer.

I recommend purchasing LTC insurance at age sixty. The older you are when you purchase it, the higher the premium will be.

Consider the cost in the long run.

- Purchase policy at age 60 for $120 per month.

- Pay on the policy for 20 years until age 80.

- Total premiums paid out of pocket are $28,800.

- Current average nursing home cost is $4,000 to $5,000 per month and likely to increase.

- The policy, if needed, will pay for itself in 6-7 months.

- If you stay in a nursing facility for 3 years with no long-term care policy, you will pay $180,000 out of pocket.

Most LTC policies will pay for nursing home, assisted living, adult daycare and home health. A LTC policy will also allow you to go to an insurance / private pay facility. You can qualify for Medicaid, but it will pay for nursing-home care *only after* your checking account is down to $2000. You can only own a home and one vehicle if using Medicaid for long-term care.

Some people think that Medicare will pay for a nursing home stay. This is not true. Medicare has a three-midnight hospital stay rule. Only after you have been in the hospital for three midnights will Medicare pay for nursing-home

care and then *only* the first one-hundred days of nursing home care; then it is up

to you to pay.  Your Medicare supplement plan or long-term disability plan will

not cover long-term care costs.

To activate LTC policy benefits, the patient must require help with at

least two of the following:

- Bathing

- Dressing

- Feeding

- Transferring to bed, chair, or toilet

- Ability to control cogency

- Help getting on/off toilet

Or the policy may be activated if a doctor states that patient needs care

for longer than ninety days due to brain injury, stroke or Alzheimer's disease.

You can get a LTC policy for a time period of three years through ten

years.  The policy time period does not begin until you draw on policy benefits.

Once the policy kicks in, you no longer pay monthly premiums.  If you die

before the age of sixty-five, your heirs receive one-hundred percent of premiums

back; some policies return one-hundred percent if you die before the age of sixty-seven. Premiums count as a medical expense and are currently tax deductible at age sixty.

The policies have elimination periods, the amount of time you pay out of pocket before the policy kicks in.

The choices are:

- 30 days

- 60 days

- 90 days

- 180 days

- or 365 days

You will also choose if you want your policy to pay a certain amount each day or each month. An example is $91 per day or $2800 per month.

When you decide which policy is best for you, the policy will have what is called "a bucket of money." When the bucket of money is gone, the policy ends. So if you have a three-year policy but at the end of three years you still have money in your bucket, the policy continues until the money is gone. Therefore, a three-year policy could actually end up lasting five or six years, depending on how the money in the bucket is spent.

Some policies offer a lifetime elimination period, which means you only meet this requirement one time. If you meet fifteen of your thirty-day period and go back home, then later you only have fifteen more days of the elimination period to meet. There is also an option of inflation protection and a rider that will waive the elimination period for Home Health. I recommend getting inflation protection.

Depending on your wealth and the inheritance you want to leave your children, it is a good idea to consider purchasing Long Term Care insurance.


## If You Can't Afford Long Term Care Insurance

If you did not get Long Term Care insurance in place or felt that you could not afford the premiums, then another option is available. Understand that Medicaid is a state-based program supplemented by government funds that provide health services only if you meet your state's poverty criteria guidelines.

Many people attempt to "spend down" their assets to state-required levels or they try to transfer assets to family members to become eligible for Medicaid. States now have the right to examine a Medicaid applicant's finances for the previous five years to determine if the applicant is eligible. Currently, in the state of Louisiana, for example, a person can qualify for Medicaid by having no more than $2,000 cash equivalent, such as money in a checking account, IRAs, stocks, bonds, and so forth. They can own a home and one vehicle. (State requirements vary, so be sure to contact your state Medicaid office for details.)

Transferring assets to a family member can be tricky. Be sure whoever you choose is handling their finances successfully, so in turn, they will handle your money correctly and not spend it. The family member has to understand that any money transferred into their name is to be used only for your care until your death. There will be expenses that have to be paid out of pocket such as clothing, haircuts, toothpaste and your day-to-day essentials.

Simply putting their name on your checking account will not work. The money has to be solely in the family member's name for five years before you qualify for Medicaid to avoid having to give back the money. If it has not cleared the five-year time period, Medicaid presumes the gifts were made to qualify for Medicaid services. This will trigger a period of ineligibility for benefits on the theory that those funds could have been used to pay for the individual's care. However, spouses may transfer assets between themselves without penalty.

In transferring assets to children, depending on the amount you decide to transfer, you may need to start early. According to the law, you can only gift a certain amount to each family member each year to avoid a gift tax. This amount changes from year to year, so consult a Certified Public Account professional for the allowable gift amount.

# Long-Term Care & Medicare

Consider this example: You have $500,000 cash above your house and car that you have worked your whole life for and want to leave some of this money to your children and grandchildren. You did not purchase Long Term Care insurance, and the time is approaching that you may need nursing home care. You may want to consider the following three options:

Option 1 is that you will pay the $200 per day, $6,000 per month out of pocket until you run out of money or die. At $6,000 per month, $72,000 per year, your $500,000 will not last long, and this option may leave no money for inheritance.

Option 2 is at approximately age 60, or any age you are comfortable, or depending on the amount you want to transfer, you start moving money to your child or children and their spouses, if you so desire (depends on the family dynamics). Be aware that no matter how well-intentioned your child may be, they could still lose the money due to bankruptcy, divorce or lawsuit. Currently, the gift amount each parent can give each child is $14,000 per year without notification to the IRS. If each parent transfers $14,000 to each of their two children, this would be $28,000 to each child and $56,000 total between the two children per year that can be transferred. Anything over that amount would be taxable by a gift tax.

Clearly, you can see that in order to transfer $500,000 at $56,000 per year, it will take about nine years and the money has to be free and clear for five years. This would mean that after the age of 74, the money would be free and clear of penalties, and you would be approved for Medicaid. This allows you to leave an advanced inheritance to your children and grandchildren. As a rule, you will want to keep enough funds in your name to pay for any care needs you may have during the resulting period of ineligibility for Medicaid and enough to maintain your present lifestyle.

Option 3 only works if you have a child who is disabled. My dear friend Debra learned this through experience. Two years ago both of her parents became very ill. They had $75,000, a house, a car, and 160 acres of land. In less than two years, their cash reserve was down to only $17,000. It was only at this time that they learned from an attorney that her parents could deed all of their assets to her brother who was disabled without recourse from the state.

A week after signing the papers, the brother then donated half of the assets to his sister Debra. Had they known this information two years earlier, they could have saved $58,000. As I stated earlier, the family dynamics have to be good in order for this to work and for the relationships not to suffer. This is a difficult subject and a challenge to figure out because you do not know when you will die. I want you to have a clear picture of your options.

## *Long-Term Care & Medicare*

You could choose not to purchase the Long Term Care or not transfer your assets, but you then run the risk of quickly spending all your money on your care, leaving nothing for inheritance. If you can afford it, I recommend getting Long Term Care insurance so this will not be a worry and you will be protected during that time of need. This is not meant to be tax advice or legal counsel; it is simply to make you aware of your options. **As you can likely tell, I feel very strongly about this topic and am seeing an increasing number of clients who are not prepared for illnesses in their older years.**

### A Quick Look at Medicare

Medicare is government health insurance for people sixty-five or older and for people under sixty-five with certain disabilities. Medicare coverage changes from time to time and you will need to check with the Medicare office, website, or your financial professional to make decisions about what is best for you.

**Medicare contact information: 1-800-medicare (1-800-633-4227) or www.medicare.gov**

The following at-a-glance information is provided as a reference but should only be used to help you consider your future and not to make major decisions about your medical coverage. Please contact the Medicare office or

149

your financial professional for up-to-date information and help figuring what works best for you.

**Medicare Part A** (Hospital Insurance)

- Inpatient care in hospitals
- Skilled nursing facility care
- Hospice care

**Medicare Part B** (Medical Insurance)

- Doctor visits
- Outpatient care
- Home Health care if medically necessary
- Durable Medical Equipment
- Some preventive services

**Medicare Part C** (Private Medicare- Medicare Advantage Plan)

- Part A & Part B combined
- Usually includes Medicare Prescription Drug (Part D)
- Cheapest premium but has out-of-pocket cost to you and *very limited* choice of doctors and hospitals

**Medicare Part D**

- Helps cover the cost of prescription drugs

- May help lower your prescription drug costs and protect against higher future costs.

The services that Medicare does not cover:

- Long Term Care -- Nursing Home Care or Custodial Home Health Care

- Routine dental or eye care

- Dentures or Cosmetic surgery

- Acupuncture

- Hearing aids and exams for fitting them

- Preventative Shingle Shot

If you are automatically enrolled, you will get your red, white and blue Medicare card in the mail three months before your sixty-fifth birthday. You will automatically get Part A and Part B on the first day of the month you turn sixty-five. (If your birthday is on the first of the month, it will start the first day of the prior month.)

**If you're drawing Social Security, you will not automatically be enrolled and you must enroll yourself.** You can sign up seven months before turning sixty-five. You will be charged a penalty if you fail to enroll on time.

The annual enrollment period is October 15 through December 7.

During this time changes can be made to your Medicare option plans, but not the supplement plans.

**\*\*Medicare premium supplements are determined by the state and zip code in which you reside.**

### Medicare Part A (Hospital Insurance)

- You usually do not pay a monthly premium for Part A coverage if you have paid into the Social Security system. However, copayments, coinsurance or deductibles may apply for each covered service.

### Medicare Part A Covered Services:

1. Inpatient care in hospitals
    - 1-60 Days you pay a $1184 deductible
    - 61-90 Days you pay $296 per day
    - 91-150 Days you pay $592 per day
2. Blood
3. Hospice care
4. Religious nonmedical health care institution
5. Skilled nursing facility care
    - 1-20 Days pays at 100%

    o   21-100 Days, you pay $148 per day

**Medicare Part B (Medical Insurance)**

- You pay a monthly premium of generally $104.90 (2013) for Part B coverage and a yearly deductible of $147, then it will pay 80/20. Premium is determined by income.

- There is no yearly limit for what you pay out-of-pocket.

- Monthly premium will be deducted from your monthly Social Security benefits.

**Medicare Part B Covered Services:**

- Abdominal aortic aneurysm screening – 1 screening only

- Alcohol misuse counseling – 1 time per year

- Ambulance services

- Ambulatory surgical centers

- Blood – charged for first 3 units in a calendar year

- Bone Density Test – 1 each 24 months

- Breast Cancer Screen Mammograms – 1 in 12 months

- Cardiac rehabilitation

- Cardiovascular disease (behavioral therapy) – 1 visit per year

- Cardiovascular screenings – 1 every 5 years

- Cervical & vaginal cancer screen – Pap test every 24 months

- Chemotherapy

- Chiropractic services – limited

- Clinical research studies

- Colorectal cancer screenings(Colonoscopy) – 1 every 10 years

- Defibrillator

- Depression screening—1 time per year

- Diabetes screenings – doctor approved 2 screenings per year

- Diabetes self-management training

- Diabetes supplies

- Doctor and other health care provider services

- Durable medical equipment (like walkers)

- EKG

- Emergency department services

- Eyeglasses – 1 pair only <u>after</u> cataract surgery

- Flu shots — 1 per year in fall or winter

- Foot exams and treatment

- Glaucoma tests – 1 each 12 months for high-risk patients

- Hearing and balance exams – if doctor ordered

# Long-Term Care & Medicare

- Hepatitis B shots – for people at high or medium risk

- HIV screening – 1 time each 12 months

- Home health services

- Kidney dialysis – 3 times per week for end stage renal disease

- Laboratory services – if doctor ordered

- Medical nutrition therapy services

- Mental health care (outpatient)

- Obesity screening and counseling

- Occupational therapy

- Outpatient hospital services

- Outpatient medical and surgical services and supplies

- Physical therapy

- Pneumococcal shot – only need once in a lifetime

- Prescription drugs – limited

- Prostate cancer screenings – once each 12 months

- Prosthetic/orthotic items

- Pulmonary rehabilitation

- Rural health clinic services

- Second surgical opinions – in some cases

- Sexually transmitted infection screenings and counseling

- Speech-language pathology services

- Surgical dressing services

- Tele-health – limited

- Tests – X-ray, MRI, CT scan, EKG – You pay 20%

- Tobacco use cessation counseling – limited

- Transplants and immunosuppressive drugs

- Yearly "Wellness" visits – after 1st year, 1 each 12 months

**Medicare Part D (Prescription Drug Coverage)**

- You pay a monthly premium for Part D coverage. You have to pick the plan that best suits your drugs. See www.medicare.gov.

**Note:** Always ask if you are being admitted into the hospital as an **Inpatient – Medicare Part A** or as an **Outpatient – Medicare Part B.**

If you are admitted as *Inpatient* – Medicare Part A, they will provide regular medication without a charge, and you will not need to bring your medication from home.

However, if you are admitted as *Outpatient* – Medicare Part B, consult the doctor about which of your maintenance medications to bring from home. Otherwise, the cost to you will be expensive. Medicare Part B does not cover maintenance medications. Anytime you are admitted as *Outpatient* – Medicare Part B pays 80/20, so you will be responsible for twenty percent of the cost.

## Chapter 12

## Leaving a Legacy Beyond Money

**A Debt-Free Tip: Life is about relationships and service, not money.**

**"For we have brought nothing into this world, so we cannot take anything out either." 1 Timothy 6:7 (New American Standard Version)**

Life is not all about the money. While that may not be what you expect to hear from a financial counselor, it is one of the most important discussions we can have. Life is about the heartfelt hope and service you can provide to others.

*What legacy are you leaving for your children? What traditions are you carrying on in your family?*

Sometimes we get so caught up in the day-to-day hustle and bustle that we don't slow down to focus on leaving something meaningful for our loved ones. It is important that we stop and take the time to consider: What kind of heritage do we want to leave our children and grandchildren?

Early in our marriage, my husband and I were told that the chances of our having children were slim. This became especially difficult as the years went on because our friends and family members having children with no problem. People would come to us with their joyful news, and, despite our happiness for

157

them, our hearts would sink. Why couldn't we get pregnant? When would it be our turn to give joyful news?

As time went by, we heard the dreaded question over and over: "When are you going to have children?" We felt we had tried everything with no success and finally started telling everyone we did not think we could have children. After many tears and prayers, we decided that if God wanted us to have a child, He would, by His timing, bless us with a child.

After six years of marriage and giving up on having a child, I went to the doctor for what I thought was a bladder infection and found out I was pregnant. We were overwhelmed with joy and thankful for this precious gift from God.

Our precious daughter was sick as a baby with Respiratory Syncytial Virus (RSV), a respiratory virus that attacks the lungs and was in and out of the hospital several times during her first year.

As new parents, it was overwhelming – financially, relationally and spiritually. After going through such a rough first year, I decided to write her a letter every year on her birthday, telling her about the year before. I wanted her to know about the good times and the tough times and what we faced together as a family.

# *Leaving a Legacy*

## How to Write a Special Letter

I simply make notes on my calendar as things happen throughout the year and refer back to my calendar to write her annual letter. When she turned one, I wrote about her being ill and how our hearts broke every time she was sick. I wrote about our love for her and our prayers for her to get well, and about how she turned our world upside down.

As she grew, each letter was different. I remember writing about how when she was three, she would ask for a piece of circle bread—her words for a hamburger bun – for a snack. If we didn't have "circle bread," she would ask for "long bread." Yep you got it: hot dog buns. I made a note of these things because I wanted to remember them.

The letters tell when she lost her first tooth, when she asked about Santa and the Easter Bunny and, yes, even when we had "The Talk." They tell of her grades, teachers and extracurricular activities. They tell of family vacations, weddings, funerals and world events, such as the September 11, 2001, terrorist attacks on the United States.

Trust me when I tell you that time does fly. It goes by faster and faster with each passing year. The importance of writing these letters each year has been impressed upon me on more than one occasion.

On one mid-December day, I was driving to the post office and a 19-year-old college student pulled out in front of me while she was texting. I was doing 55 mph and had *no* brake time. Both vehicles were totaled, and we both went to the hospital.

I have to pause right here and say: **"Please, do not text and drive."**

OMG = TRGDY; don't do it.

With a badly bruised sternum, two cut knees, a chipped elbow and a hurt shoulder, it became clear to me that the Lord could have taken me home to be with Him that very day.

Although I ended up having knee and shoulder surgery, I survived that accident because of a seat belt, an airbag and the grace of God. However, if it would have been my time to go, my daughter would have had thirteen handwritten letters telling her how much she was loved and how proud I was to be her mom. No matter how old she is, she will have those letters from her parents, and I know they will be a gift that no amount of money could replace.

A colleague shared his experience regarding the importance of a letter as well. He and his late wife wrote letters to each of their three children just prior to embarking on a trip to Japan. Almost fourteen years later, she died suddenly in an automobile accident. Those letters are held tightly and cherished by each of the children.

## Leaving a Legacy

My father has a letter written by his father to his mother while he was fighting for the United States during World War II and she was at home raising three small children, two boys and a girl. At the end of that letter, my grandfather told my grandmother, "Kiss the babies for me, and I love you." My father holds that letter close to his heart, as I and my daughter will one day.

No amount of money can provide that personal touch of a written gift.

My uncle Don, "Pappa D," is a pastor who writes a letter to the babies born in his church congregation telling them about their first day at church. He recounts how they were dressed, what type of day it was and how happy and excited everyone was to see them. He tells how incredibly proud their parents are to have them as their son or daughter and what a bright future they have. He presents the sealed letter to the parents at the time of the baby's dedication and asks the parents to open it and read it to the child on his or her twelfth birthday. He chose twelve because that was the age when Jesus came to the temple. Twelve is a significant number in a lot of different ways, including the time a boy or girl transitions from childhood into adulthood.

Perhaps Pappa D got his love of letters from his grandmother, "Maw Maw" Woodard, who loved nothing more than getting a letter in the mail. She always said that when a phone call is over, it is over, but a letter can be read over, and over, and over again.

When she received a letter from her sister in Houston, Texas, she would read it as she walked slowly down the hot sandy road from the mailbox back to the house. She would then read it again before going to bed that night and read it throughout the week. The power and ability that words on paper have to touch the heart is truly amazing.

After writing to our daughter on her birthday, I place the letter in a fireproof lock box. These letters will one day serve as a documentary of her life as a child and of our life as a family.

It is my plan to give her the first letter on the day her first child is born, so she will be able to read about things that she did in the first twelve months of her life. I hope that these letters will guide her and help her in raising her child and keep her from feeling alone because we all know children *do not* come with a manual.

If life unfolds as I pray it will, I will give her the second letter on the first birthday of her child and so on until her child turns twenty, hopefully providing her with a helpful manual about child-rearing. Once our daughter turns twenty-one, I will start giving her the letters in real time, telling her about the year before. If she is unable to have children or chooses not to have children, then the first twenty letters will be given to her on her fortieth birthday.

# *Leaving a Legacy*

The letters will not be given to her during her teenage years—just in case she has a bad day and decides she doesn't want them. If you have ever had a teenager, you understand their occasional outbursts and rolling of the eyes along with sometimes rash decisions they make during this time of growth.

Writing these letters is a legacy that every parent can provide for their child or grandparent to do for their grandchildren. You can start this at any age. Who doesn't want a handwritten letter from their mom or dad? And if you don't want to handwrite the letter, type it, print it on fun paper and sign it.

It is sad to me that this cherished art has fallen by the wayside with texting and technology, but we can change that. We are only here for a very short time. Don't wait; write a letter today.

Below you will find excerpts from two letters I wrote to our daughter. The first I wrote on beautiful flowered stationery with music symbols for her first birthday. I felt so blessed to have been given a daughter that I was moved to tell her how much she was loved and appreciated by us.

The second is the letter written on her thirteenth birthday telling about her year as a sixth grader. At the time I wrote this letter, the thought of writing a book was like taking a trip to Mars. I guess it goes to show that you never know the plans God has for you.

**Excerpt from first letter:**

Dear Doodle Bug,                    Thursday, September 7, 1999

We want you to know that you are our gift from God. You have brought us so much love and happiness. It is truly amazing how much you have grown in just one year! Every day is a new adventure that you pursue with such strength and courage. We have been blessed with the opportunity to love, teach and care for you. Your birthday party is on this Saturday and we are busy getting ready for it. Daddy and I bought you your first piano since you love music so much. For now, your favorite type of music is classical – you always insist that we listen to that CD anytime we are in the car. I hope you like the stationery that I chose to write on I thought it went well with your gift and love for music.

Despite being so ill, you are always smiling and everyone always says what a happy baby you are. Daddy and I have really had to go through some adjustments for me to quit work and stay at home with you, but it has all been worth it. I only wish I could be the one sick and not you. It breaks our hearts to see you struggle but every day you continue to amaze us.

We thank God every day for choosing us to be your parents. You took your first steps at 11 months. You have already started talking and your first words were "Daddy" and "EE'EE" (Prissy-our Pomeranian).

# *Leaving a Legacy*

I love to hear you giggle when daddy is playing with Prissy and making her bark. Well, you will be waking up soon from your nap and I just wanted to write you a note saying "Happy 1st Birthday" and we want you to forever grow up each day knowing in your heart how much we as your parents LOVE YOU!

Always,

Mommy & Daddy


**Excerpt from fifth letter:**


Dear Daughter,                                    September 8, 2003

Kindergarten – this does not seem possible. It was just last September that you started preschool in Walker, Louisiana.

On October 2, 2002, Hurricane Lili was headed for Lafayette, LA. at a speed of close to 200 mph, so we had to pack up all of our valuables in our cars and drive to north Louisiana for safety. It is a scary feeling to drive away from your home not knowing if it will be there when you return. We were very lucky and had minimal damage from the storm.

On January 15, 2003, we found out that we were being transferred again to Ruston, Louisiana. It took us until August to sell the house and to get moved. It worked out because you were able to finish preschool and dance class for the year. God's timing is the best; He may not be early but He is never late! We arrived in Ruston just in time for you to start your kindergarten year.

**Excerpt from twelfth letter:**

Our Dearest Girl,                                    September 7, 2011

Happy Birthday Teenager- 13

This past year you were a cheerleader and seemed to really enjoy it. Sixth grade year was busy but you did a good job of keeping your grades up, which always makes us very proud. You are such a smart girl and we know you have great potential to become whatever God intends for you to become.

On the very cold rainy morning of December 16, 2010 at 8:52 I received a call from the Radiology Department of the clinic. The lady was calling to tell me that on the mammogram I had done the week before, they found a lump in my left breast and that I needed to come back in for more films. I literally could not breathe when I hung up the phone and felt like I had been kicked in the stomach. Only five months earlier your dad had open heart surgery, heart valve replacement and triple bypass, and now this.

I went back in on December 22$^{nd}$ for more films and we were planning to leave on the 23$^{rd}$ for Nanny & Paw Paw's for Christmas. The lady told me that they had bad news and worse news. The bad news was that they found the lump in my left breast but the worse news was that it was up against the back chest wall which makes it harder to treat. They did more films, an ultrasound, and a biopsy. About a week later the test confirmed that I did not have breast cancer. It was a life changing moment for me.

I do believe that everything happens for a reason and strongly felt like God knows that I do public speaking and I could tell this story to others and possibly save someone's life. So now at the end of each seminar I encourage all women to get their mammograms and all men to get their prostate exams **yearly**. It had been 3 years since my previous exam but I learned not to wait and promise that I will get it every year from now on, no matter how busy or crazy life gets.

There is a picture that now hangs in the hallway outside of our bedroom that reminds me every day of this experience. The picture says, "The Will of God will never take you where the Grace of God will not Protect You." I believe this is for past, present, and future.

On March 23, 2011 Memok and Granddaddy were married for 60 years. How awesome is that? Pretty amazing, I think.

On August 19th you started your first day of junior high school and really liked it. You like having a locker and getting to change classes this year. You do have your plate full with all honors classes, GT art and cheerleading but I know you can do it. We have great confidence in you. I don't know if I have ever mentioned to you or not but I pray every day. My prayer time is usually in the mornings while in the bath tub. It provides me with the comfort to start the day. God is so good!

I pray the following for you each day:

Physical, emotional, and spiritual health

An abiding sense of safety and security

Courage to face the problems of each day

A calm spirit to hear the voice of the Lord

A willingness to obey

A clear mind, both to learn and to recall

A generous spirit toward family and friends

Wise teachers, mentors and counselors

An unshakable self-worth and personal dignity

Your future spouse

Your Salvation

It is amazing how time seems to fly by faster and faster the older you get. Just know that we are very proud of you and love you deeply with all of our heart and forever only want the very, very best for you. I pray every day for God's will for your life and for your future husband whoever God has for you.

We love you, we love you, we love you......

## *Leaving a Legacy*

She knows I write her these letters. I think the act of writing letters has sparked her interest because at age fifteen, several days before Christmas, she decided she wanted to write a letter to each of her grandparents telling them how much she loved and admired them. She placed each letter in a sealed envelope and instructed her grandparents not to open the letters until Christmas morning.

**The letter below is the letter that was written to her grandmother, who was eighty-three years old at the time.**

Dear Memok,                                    December 19, 2013

I admire you so much. I tend to take for granted what a special woman you truly are. I am blessed to have you as my grandmother. When I asked you what you wanted for Christmas, you couldn't think of anything. Your modesty shows a quality of a hero in a book. I once read about a woman, graceful and humble, who waited 20 years for her husband to return from war. She was a quiet, patient, kind hearted woman, just like you.

I must say that if I had a hero, you would be it. One day I hope to be as kind as you are. I hope to be as smart and charismatic as you are too. I still remember waking up at your house and you would be in the kitchen making me Mickey Mouse pancakes while I was watching morning cartoons. I remember in

Kindergarten when I opened my box of raisins and there was an unexpected friendly worm inside. That was a great day.

I also remember when we had a family get together and I went outside to pick you some flowers and picked all of your good irises. I didn't know not to pick them but you didn't mind at all. Those are memories that can never be replaced and will be forever cherished.

This Christmas I am giving you this letter to show how much I care. I know that people grow older, but never will I grow apart from you. I love you so dearly.

You have always been patient, cheerful, kind and loving. Thank you for being the most amazing grandmother anyone could ever ask for.

Your loving granddaughter,


I am sure you can imagine how overjoyed her grandmother was after reading this letter from her youngest granddaughter. No amount of money can buy that!

Don't wait.

What letter will you write today?

# Chapter 13

**Add Your Name to Those Living the Debt-Free Dream**

**A Debt-Free Tip: Sacrifice to win. It is worth it.**

**"In the house of the wise are stores of choice food and oil,**

**but a foolish man devours all he has."**

**Proverbs 21:20 (New International Version)**


This is it. The time is now. You can do it! Add your name to those who are living the Debt-Free & Wealthy dream. Just like words have great power and ability, so do numbers and having a financial plan that works. I hope you have walked with me through the step-by-step process to successfully manage your money. Take heart from these people below – real people, just like you and I, who have done this program and are living the Debt-Free & Wealthy dream.

Below you will read testimonials from clients from different walks of life and different backgrounds. Everyone faces financial challenges throughout life. These people have given permission to have their personal stories published because they want to give hope to others who want to succeed financially.

**Overwhelmed? ...consider this**

"My name is Shirley and I just want to say 'thank you.' I attended the Financial Wellness event at the Convention Center offered by Centric Federal Credit Union. I just wanted to share that I didn't know how much financial trouble I was in until I attended the event. I sat there and wondered if there was any hope for me. I scheduled an appointment with Kelly and embarrassingly laid out all my monthly income and expenses. Needless to say, my expenses outweighed my income by a large margin. This Financial Wellness program has helped me to cut back on a lot of things and I must say that I do feel that there may be hope for me after all.

Thank you so much to the Centric Federal Credit Union for offering such an opportunity to allow someone to reach out to those of us who didn't know that such help was available. But most importantly, that help could be offered from a trustworthy, Christian person. I am grateful and I hope that my testimony may help someone else realize that there is hope even when we may not see it. I am so glad to be a member of your credit union and to have been given this opportunity. This is better than any loan I could ever get.

You never know how many people you are helping. Thank you a million times over."

– Shirley – 2012

# *Living the Debt-Free Dream*

## Three kids and what to do?

"This lady might just be one of my most favorite people of all time. Because of her one-on-one guidance, we are preparing for our future. If anyone wants to learn the most wonderful way to manage their finances, she and this book is the answer. Even if you don't have any debt, she teaches you how to save, invest, manage money, etc.

With 3 girls, 3 future college tuitions, and 3 weddings...We had to get this saving thing under control. And let me tell you, if I can do this program ANYONE can do this program. She is certified through Dave Ramsey, and goes into more detail about how to achieve the things he teaches. I highly recommend this wonderful, sweet, smart, talented lady. Having her for a financial advisor was one of the wisest decisions we have ever made. Her fee is so small compared to money success you will receive through this program. You are the best, Kelly Brantley. We are looking forward to learning more and more from you!" – Mattieu & Kristen - 2014

### Not temporary, but a lifestyle change

My wife and I have just completed the first month of our new budget and are amazed. It has been an eye opening experience putting a name to every dollar that we make. Not only does it give you peace of mind, but also assurance that day by day you are getting closer to financial freedom. After our first meeting with Kelly, it became very clear that she was doing what God put her on this earth to do.

She is *awesome*. Not only does she assure you there is hope for your future, she connects with you on a personal level with stories of her own financial struggles. This program is not temporary, but a lifestyle change!

– Matt & Michelle - 2013

## Paid off vehicles

Kelly is an amazing lady to work with. She truly knows and understands where her clients are coming from and exactly how to get them to where they want to be. I highly recommend working with her. Since 2011 we have paid off our vehicles and we are looking forward to building a new home this year (2013). We wouldn't be here today without Kelly's help.

– Jason & Shanna – 2011

## Debt-Free Including the Home

What an amazing journey this has been the last 21 months. Kay stopped working full time in August 2008 to work at home and help take care of her mother who was recovering from a broken hip. We felt that we had a good income, but we have always struggled to maintain a savings account and to have money left over at the end of the month.

Kelly had invited Kay and I to join her class in January 2008, but we were too busy to take the class. By October 2008, Kay was not working, but we were still living the same lifestyle we had always lived, with $92,000 of debt and only one income. All of a sudden we woke up and realized we were not going to make our expenses that month. This was a HUGE wake-up call for us. We had to change our lifestyle.

We immediately signed up for the January 2009 class. Through weekly discussions (encouragement and focus sessions) with Kelly and other classmates, we began making changes. We set a goal to become debt-free, other than our mortgage, in two years. We immediately sold Kay's Lexus and focused on paying off the credit card, but had no savings. After establishing an Emergency Fund, we became focused on debt and cash flow.

To meet our goal, we realized that we needed to sell our herd of cattle that we had spent 6+ years building up. This money went to pay off a pickup,

(2) tractors, and a cow loan. Although it was difficult, we can now say that it was the best investment we ever made. In just 21 months, we have a 4 month Emergency Fund with an additional savings account and are now DEBT-FREE, other than our mortgage.

We are now buying cattle again, but now it is on a cash-basis only. We have needed and wanted a workshop on this farm but our new goal is to pay off our mortgage in less than 3 years, with a stretch goal of two years. God continues to bless us every day. It was only through our faith and trust in Him that we were able to make the necessary changes to our lifestyle.

Kelly, we cannot thank you enough for all of your help and encouragement. Your heart and passion for helping others comes through every time we talk.

– Paul & Kay – 2009

**Update:** *We Did It!* As of February 2013, we are now completely Debt Free – including our home.

## We *were* the Norm...

In January 2008, my husband and I took our first financial class with Kelly. Little did we know that it would change our lives forever. We were the "norm." We were paying our bills and were current, but we had too much month at the end of our money and living from paycheck to paycheck. We decided that we'd had enough of being "normal." Dave Ramsey talks about finding someone with the heart of a teacher and Kelly is just that. She loves helping others and will work with you until you understand the process.

My husband and I got intense and paid a lot of our debt down. We have money in savings now. We paid off two vehicle loans. We no longer are living paycheck to paycheck. It is a crock pot process, and in January 2009, we decided to sit through Kelly's class again because I felt that we had lost some of our intensity. Going through the class again gave us the boost that we needed.

We have no credit card debt and we have cut up the credit cards. No more living on plastic. I cannot begin to tell you how living on a budget and not paying credit card debt has given us such a peace of mind. It feels wonderful! I truly believe that we will always make wise decisions when it comes to money. Thank you, Kelly, from the bottom of our hearts for what you have done for us and have taught us. You truly love what you do and with the love of a teacher.

– Richard and Salli – 2008

# Living the Debt-Free Dream

## New Life – New Beginning

Kelly, I cannot tell you how excited we are about this *New Beginning!* We honestly had no idea what to do as far as paying our debt off and finding financial stability for our family, but you have taught us how to get there. I was fighting back tears of joy when you were showing us how things will be in our financial future just by following the plan. It is so exciting to actually see on paper what our financial future holds for us.

I truly believe that God puts people in your life for a reason, and His reason for you is quite clear....to lead us in the right direction to start our *new* life. We can't thank you enough for all you have done. You have a true calling in life, and wow, what a blessing! We love you truly and we will be calling you in the near future to keep you updated on our success.

– Brad and Holly – 2013

179

### Paying off student loans

Student Loan #1 has been paid in full all thanks to this program! Thanks Kelly Brantley for the motivation and guidance. Now on to Student Loan #2 and being Debt-Free with Kelly. (www.debtfreewithkelly.com)

– Ashley – 2013

### Not good with money?

I am just not good with money. Some people are good with money and some aren't and I am one of the latter. This was the lie I had been telling myself my entire life. I was 31 years old, living paycheck to paycheck and drowning in debt, and I thought it was the norm. It was normal to struggle. It was normal to have debt for your entire life. It was normal to decline 1-800 calls from collection agencies on a daily basis. It was normal to lie awake at night and wonder how I was going to make it through the month.

Then, one day, I saw a friend's post on Facebook how she had paid $10,000 off of her student loan debt in one year after working with Kelly. Without even thinking, I simply picked up the phone and called this Kelly person and set up an appointment. After meeting with her and learning about the program, the next step was writing down all of my monthly bills and debt and this was by far the scariest part. For so long, I was able to avoid all things money.

## *Living the Debt-Free Dream*

When the next meeting came and I had to say out loud how much money I owed, I equated it to walking into the room and stripping down all of my clothes for someone to see...with a high beam spotlight. However, Kelly worked her magic and came back with what I now refer to as my money manual. She broke down how and when to pay my bills, but not only pay my electricity, rent, etc. but to start paying on that dreaded student loan and pay back more than my monthly payment.

I was scared that I wasn't going to be able to have any fun, or God forbid, not be able to buy any more Icees. But there was weekend money and "Me Money" built into each week. I even had it in my budget to be able to put money in savings and give part of my pay to my church. So, here I was thinking I barely had enough money to scrape by and Kelly had me GIVING money back? I simply followed the "manual" week by week. Each month, my savings account grew. Each month, my debt went down. Each month, the pit in my stomach went further and further away.

I remember calling her after the first month, and saying, "Kelly, what in the world have I been spending money on?" I never thought I was able to pay all of my bills, pay off my debts, save money and give back. I am only six months into the program but I have a whole new attitude about money and about life. This was THE best decision I have ever made and I have never felt so free.

There is not a constant dark cloud following me around, making me worry about having debt, or worry about not having money set aside for an emergency.

I think it is such a gift to be able to provide someone with stability and peace of mind and I literally thank God on a regular basis that I picked up the phone to call Kelly. While I am not debt free - *yet* - I am definitely free of worry, stress, and tension when it comes to money and could not be more thankful!

– Ashley – 2014

# *Living the Debt-Free Dream*

### No credit card, CASH payment only

We are so thankful for your teachings. A couple of days ago we received a letter in the mail from our mortgage company stating that our escrow account will soon be short $1461.00 due to a tax and insurance increase. The mortgage company also stated that we had 30 days to pay this shortage or our mortgage payment would increase by a whopping $200.00 per month. But thanks to your teachings and this awesome plan we have the cash in hand and will not have to even consider putting it on a credit card. It seems as if every week we have extra money left over in our envelopes, it is amazing.

When I opened the letter from the mortgage company, there was no panic attack. I showed it to Alex. He said we will just write the check and life will go on stress free. Thank God for sending you our way! If it weren't for you this would have been another charge on a credit card instead of a CASH payment. We are so grateful. Thank you.

– Alex and Kenya – 2014

**Aloha from Hawaii**

I just wanted to say thank you. We have paid off the $14,632 in student loans and our house in the states is under contract and should close in September. We have saved $30,000 since we started budgeting. You are wonderful and I cannot thank you enough.

– Dallas & Crystal – 2014

**Moving….**

Steve and I wanted to check in with you and let you know how we are doing. We've made the move to Shreveport, Louisiana and have been here for almost a month now. We found a nice apartment in a good neighborhood for $50 less than what you told us we could spend on housing and the good thing is that

# *Living the Debt-Free Dream*

Internet is included. We have also found that our utilities are much lower than our rent house that we had in Ruston.

We have also decided to take your advice about our dogs. We were able to find good homes for all three Great Danes. That was the hardest thing I have ever done, but I know it was the wisest decision. Now we are saving the $100 per month on pet expenses, and the house is easier to keep clean.

We are still following our plan and paying off debt. It is slow going but we are sticking to it and should have one more paid off in December. Steve's student loan has been moved out of the collections department and into the loan rehabilitation department thanks to your help. We should be through the rehabilitation program in February. Our jobs are going well and Steve just got a raise (Wahoo). Thank you so much for all you have done for us. The tools you have given us have changed our lives. Now we can't even imagine living without a money plan.

**Update** – Because of you we have been saving for a car that we knew we would soon have to purchase. After several months, my car died and it was time to purchase another one. We had $3100 saved and ended up buying a 2002 Subaru Forester for $3000. I cannot tell you how great it felt to have the cash to pay for the car up front. Also we just wrote another payoff check last month. Goodbye Discover Card!

Well…even with all the little bumps in the road of life, we have still managed to purchase a home and pay off all of our debt except for Steve's student loan, which we continue to pay down each month. Once again, thank you for all of your help. Thank you. Thank you. Thank you. Your ministry truly changes lives.

– Steve & Jesse – 2008

### Beating Cancer

I am so glad that I talked to Kelly about two months ago. Literally, our conversation has changed my coaching along with my personal life. I really felt previously like my coaching only helped a few of my clients, which disturbed me. So I began praying, and Kelly was the answer.

Now after implementing the budgets the way that she teaches, I now have happy and satisfied clients. Moreover, it has certainly made me happier to know that I am helping my clients more.

Kelly did not know this at the time, but my wife, Kelli, was diagnosed with breast cancer (doctors do think that they got it all) a few months back so she was not able to work her regular hours. But partially because of Kelly's help, I have been able to take on an extra work load. So, here's to another life that Kelly has changed!

– Brad – Dave Ramsey Financial Coach, New Orleans, Louisiana

"You make me so proud! The question of the day…how many lives can one woman change? The answer? **Another One!**

– Les Nienow – Dave Ramsey 'Financial Coach' Specialist – Nashville, TN

These are a few of many personal success stories. You can do it, too. I know you can because I have seen ordinary people like you pay off huge debts. Do not quit. Don't look back and keep moving forward. Believe in yourself. I do! This program works one day at a time, one step at a time and one dollar at a time. That is how we get to where we are going. Continue pushing yourself. Read and re-read until you understand the tools that will bring you Financial Freedom.

I received this email from a thirty-four year old engaged client who is ready to start his life personally and financially: "Things are going great and I am really excited about how easy this plan has become once I got used to it. It feels great not to have to sweat out waiting for paydays anymore." On my desk and at all of my Financial Wellness seminars I pass out lifesavers as a snack. The lifesavers serve as a symbol that this program truly did save my life spiritually, relationally, and financially. I am not saying that any of this is going to be easy, but in the end it will be worth it because you will feel and experience the reward of being Debt-Free with Kelly and the reward of building wealth. You *can* be Debt-Free & Wealthy!

# Chapter 14

## Discussion Questions for a Six-Week Study

**A Debt-Free Tip: Be humble and apply this knowledge to your life.**

**"Therefore wisdom and knowledge will be given you. And I will also give you wealth, riches and honor, such as no king who was before you ever had and none after you will have."**

**2 Chronicles 1:12 (New International Version)**

Perhaps you would enjoy being part of a group study about money. You can enjoy this study with a group of friends, a group of church members, a group of men, or a group of women. Or you simply may decide to study the discussion questions alone or with your partner. By working your way through the tools taught in this book and the discussion questions, you will be left with more financial knowledge than before. Knowledge is power, and this book is an investment in knowledge for your family's financial future. Do not to let this overwhelm you. Walk this financial journey "One Dollar at a Time to Be Debt-Free & Wealthy."

## Week 1- Chapter 1 & 2

### Chapter 1 – Relationships – Can't Live With Them, Can't Live Without Them

1. How would you describe your characteristics in dealing with money?
2. What character traits best describe your spouse or partner in dealing with money?
3. How do you communicate about money? Why?
4. In what ways did you see your parents handle money? Are you the same or different?
5. In what ways do you see God validating your dreams?
6. How did you relate to this chapter? What changes might you make?

### Chapter 2 – The Heaviness of Debt

1. What physical symptoms have you experienced due to the stress of debt?
2. What sacrifice can you make to get out of debt and what rewards might you gain from your sacrifice?
3. Do you know anyone who had filed bankruptcy? How did it affect his or her life?
4. In what order should debts be listed on the scratch-off debt list and why?
5. How could being Debt-Free with Kelly change your life?

# *Discussion Questions*

## Week 2 - Chapter 3 & 4

### Chapter 3 – The Envelope Please:  Learning to Pay with Cash

1.  How might the envelopes work for your family?
2.  Which envelope are you most excited about using?  Why?
3.  What activities do you plan to spend your weekend money for?
4.  What type of items do you plan to purchase with your Me Money?
5.  Do you use cash or debit card for the fuel envelope?  Why?
6.  How often should you fill all of your envelopes?

### Chapter 4 – Learning to Set Money Aside for Non-Monthly Expenses that Surprise Us

1.  What is an example of non-monthly categories you will use in your family?
2.  How can planning monthly for non-monthly expenses help your family?
3.  How will saving each month for Christmas and Gifts help you budget?
4.  Why is it important to budget Christmas and Gifts separately?
5.  Why is having a utility category a good idea?

## Week 3 – Chapter 5 & 6

### Chapter 5 – Step by Step to a Debt-Free Life

1. Why is it a good idea to use your net pay instead of your gross pay when doing a budget?
2. If your paycheck varies, how much income should be used in the budget?
3. In what order should the items be listed on the scratch-off debt list? Why?
4. On what day do you fill your envelopes? Why?
5. What budget information might you gather?

### Chapter 6 – Building a Debt-Free Plan that Works

1. How does Proverbs 24:27 speak to you?
2. How will you run your friendly distribution sheet? Why?
3. If you are paid weekly, how many 4 week months are there in a year and how many 5 week months are there in a year?
4. If you are paid biweekly, how many 4 week months are there in a year and how many 6 week months will you have in a year?
5. How does the credit card trap make you feel? How might you get out of that trap?

*Discussion Questions*

**Week 4 – Chapter 7 & 8**

**Chapter 7 – Let It Flow:  The Secret to Having Enough Money**

1.   What is the secret to having enough money and a financial plan that works?
2.   How can a flow number be beneficial to your budget?
3.   Is the flow number used at the beginning of the budget the same number at the end of the budget?  Why?
4.   Discuss your options if your expenses are higher than your income. How may you make situation better?
5.   What small steps can you make in improving how to pay your bills?

**Chapter 8 – How to Pay Cash for a Car:  The Best Kept Financial Success Secret**

1.   What does scripture say about cosigning?
2.   What is the recommended amount to save each month to pay cash for a car?
3.   Are vehicles a good investment or a bad investment?  Why?
4.   How much do vehicles depreciate in the first four years?
5.   What changes might you make in your vehicles to save money?

## Week 5 – Chapter 9 & 10

### Chapter 9 – Learning to Pay Off Student Loans

1. Are student loans bankruptable?
2. How much money should students borrow for school loans? Why?
3. What happens to the interest when student loans are deferred?
4. What percentage of your wages can be garnished for student loans? Do they have to give you notice of garnishment?
5. How will it benefit you to research college costs and career choice before enrolling?
6. What gift and service do you think God has given you to provide to others?

### Chapter 10 – Saving, Investing and Retirement…It *IS* Closer Than You Think

1. How early should you start saving for retirement?
2. Why is the Roth IRA better than a Traditional IRA?
3. Which IRA grows tax free? How much can you withdraw without penalty?
4. What are you doing to teach your children about saving money?
5. How can it benefit your family for you to make an appointment with the Social Security office after turning 50 years old?

# Discussion Questions

## Week 6 – Chapter 11 & 12

### Chapter 11 – Understanding Long Term Care & Medicare

1. What are the requirements to activate a Long Term Care policy?
2. How much money can you have in a checking account when you qualify for Medicaid?
3. Discuss with your spouse or partner which option is best for your family.
4. When is the best time to start planning for your elderly care?
5. Discuss the difference between Medicare part A, B, C, & D.

### Chapter 12 – Leaving a Legacy Beyond Money

1. What experiences have shown you that life is not all about money?
2. Who might you like to write a letter to?
3. What are some traditions your family practices?
4. How does receiving a letter from a friend or family member make you feel?
5. What legacy will you leave beyond money?

# About the Author

Kelly Brantley was born in New Orleans, Louisiana, and graduated from Louisiana Tech University with a degree Business Management. She became a Dave Ramsey Certified Counselor in March 2008 and became a small-business owner when she opened Financial Freedom Counseling Service in January 2009. In addition to her experience in financial coaching, she has management experience in human resources in the manufacturing and health care industries.

A nationally known financial expert, Kelly appears bi-weekly on KNOE TV 8 giving money tips to viewers and speaks frequently to groups. She has spoken to thousands of families about how to become Debt-Free & Wealthy one dollar at a time. She also has worked with employers to bring Financial Wellness to their employees and assisted families nationwide in putting together individual financial and wealth building plans. Her message is inspirational, practical, and unique. Best of all, as her thousands of clients and seminar participants attest, it works!

Kelly lives in Louisiana with her husband of 21 years and their daughter. They enjoy the outdoors, football and family time.

If you are interested in having Kelly address your organization or conduct a Financial Wellness Seminar or wish to receive more information about one-on-one coaching for your family:

E-mail - debtfreewithkelly@gmail.com

or

Write - P.O. Box 2295, Ruston, LA  71273-2295

or

Visit Her Website - www.debtfreewithkelly.com.